# HOW BULIMIA SAVED MY SOUL

## A NOVEL

Welland Andrus

Trilogy Christian Publishers
A Wholly Owned Subsidiary of Trinity Broadcasting Network
2442 Michelle Drive
Tustin, CA 92780

Copyright © 2020 by Welland Andrus

All Scripture quotations, unless otherwise noted, taken from THE HOLY BIBLE, NEW INTERNATIONAL VERSION®, NIV® Copyright © 1973, 1978, 1984, 2011 by Biblica, Inc.® Used by permission. All rights reserved worldwide.

Scripture quotations marked (KJV) taken from *The Holy Bible, King James Version*. Cambridge Edition: 1769.

All rights reserved, including the right to reproduce this book or portions thereof in any form whatsoever.

For information, address Trilogy Christian Publishing
Rights Department, 2442 Michelle Drive, Tustin, Ca 92780.
Trilogy Christian Publishing/ TBN and colophon are trademarks of Trinity Broadcasting Network.

For information about special discounts for bulk purchases, please contact Trilogy Christian Publishing.

Manufactured in the United States of America

Trilogy Disclaimer: The views and content expressed in this book are those of the author and may not necessarily reflect the views and doctrine of Trilogy Christian Publishing or the Trinity Broadcasting Network.

10 9 8 7 6 5 4 3 2 1

Library of Congress Cataloging-in-Publication Data is available.

ISBN 978-1-64773-550-0 (Print Book)
ISBN 978-1-64773-551-7 (ebook)

For Mariah.
Thank you for encouraging me to chase my dream.

For Kayla and Hannah.
Thank you for running with me on the way there.

For my wonderful grandparents Claire and Richard Andrus.
Thank you for always supporting me and my
dreams. I wouldn't be here without you.

# PREFACE

## Author's Note

When I was seventeen, I was sent to Princeton for treatment of bulimia nervosa. According to the National Eating Disorders Association, *bulimia* is defined as "a serious, potentially life-threatening eating disorder characterized by a cycle of bingeing and compensatory behaviors such as self-induced vomiting designed to undo or compensate for the effects of binge eating."

I struggled with eating disorders from when I was in eighth grade all the way to when I was a freshman in college. I had the idea for this book when I was in tenth grade of high school and finished planning and making the ideas for it when I was in treatment. I want to show someone from the outside looking in the emotions someone struggling could feel and how it's more than just someone who doesn't want to eat.

I want it to be known to the reader that the following story can be triggering for some readers and triggering for someone who is in the middle of the struggle. This book uses numbers (such as weight and height). It also goes into explicit details on the symptoms of bulimia. I would advise someone who is struggling to not jump into this book right away if they don't feel like they're in the step in their recovery yet. This book shows what someone struggling with an eating disorder might feel and what the deadly cycle of bulimia looks like. I want the reader to be aware that there are things in this book leading up to someone getting saved (drinking, eating disorders, doubt of God, etc.). All these things help the main character get saved. If you struggle with any of these, I want to encourage you to seek God. He loves you and cares about you. The Bible says He will *never* leave or forsake you.

I didn't feel comfortable writing my own story yet, but what I did do is make a story that is loosely based on mine and not only what eating disorders did to me but also what it did to my family members surrounding me and how I felt from looking out. I also want to encourage the reader that if you are struggling, please get help. There's no shame in telling on yourself, and there is no shame in admitting you have a problem. Your family and friends love you more than you will ever understand, and our God and Jesus Christ loves you unconditionally.

God bless you, my friends, and thank you for reading.

# PROLOGUE

## Winter of 2024

There's something about a drive alone in the middle of a cold night. You, the road, the comfortable feeling of the heat beating the windshield, keeping the frost from freezing over top of it. The songs that hit you in the heart playing on the stereo from either your aux cord or Bluetooth. It's all comforting, the reason you're out driving that late to begin with. That was where I was at 1:43 a.m., twenty-one degrees outside, driving my truck while one of my favorite songs or artists played on Pandora, the heat hitting my face to keep me from freezing over, the windshield wipers going to push the snow away as it hit.

    I just got a new job as the pastor at Rising Hope Community Church in southern Massachusetts. After my over-the-phone interview and a few days of rest, I grabbed my belongings and started driving from New Jersey to Massachusetts. I was expected to arrive around 4:00 a.m., which only left me a couple of hours and one more stop at a gas station before I reached my destination. It was only a seven-hour drive, but I wanted to leave early to beat the snow and to have a couple of days to explore my new town before meeting my new board members face-to-face. At least I'd get a couple of days. A new job, a change of scenery, and a job as a lead pastor at age twenty-four—I couldn't beat it, right?

"We have a house for you to stay in," Bill from the church had said over the phone after I got hired. "It's definitely not the most glamorous house. The church owns it, and it's in the woods. The last pastor bought it so he'd have peace to write his sermons. You're free to stay in it until you get your own place, if you chose to, anyway."

I stopped for gas about twenty minutes before reaching the house and to grab one more cup of coffee to hold me over before I could get to sleep. The snow was really starting to get bad. But I was almost to the house. I sucked up the freezing temperature and ran into the store at the gas station to get that cup of coffee while the gas pumped.

"You must be moving somewhere," the girl behind the counter said.

"How did you know?" I asked.

She started nodding at the window toward my truck. "Jersey plates, it's almost four in the morning, and the snow is coming down hard. No one would travel this far up north in these conditions for any other reason. Lucky guess?"

"I'll give that one to you," I said, chuckling.

"How much farther of a drive do you have?"

"Actually, only twenty minutes at the speed I'm driving. I just wanted to fill up and get more caffeine in me so I wouldn't have to tomorrow."

"Good idea," she said. "Well, welcome to Massachusetts! I'm Celest."

"Larry," I said, shaking her hand, then giving her the money for the gas and coffee.

"Well, you better get to wherever you're going. But maybe I'll see you around sometime?" she said, smiling.

"You bet," I said. Then walking toward the exit, I put my hood back up and walked out into the cold.

Driving slowly yet as safely as I could, I made it to the house. It was on a good piece of land in the woods and only a ten-minute drive away from the church I'd be working at. Not bad at all. When I got to the house, I got my leather bag full of blankets and some clothes and ran toward the house. I'd get the rest of my belongings after getting a decent amount of sleep. I just had a long drive and didn't want to unpack after it was all over.

The living room lights were already on. The second I walked into the house, I saw a living room with one couch, a recliner chair, and a fireplace with a TV hanging over it. There wasn't a wall separating the living room from the kitchen, though the wood floor of the living room ended with the tiled floor of the kitchen, and there was a bar that extended across most of the dividing floor. Walking toward the bar, I went and saw a new coffeepot with a pie sitting next to it. On top of the pie there was a message:

*Larry,*

*Welcome to Massachusetts and your new home!*
*Enjoy this pie baked by the church and get yourself comfortable. We are looking forward to seeing you Saturday morning to discuss plans for the church and what ideas you have for us.*
*—Bill*

On the far end of the kitchen, there was a small room with a washer, dryer, and a door leading into the backyard. There was another opening on the other side of the living room; it opened to a roomy office space with a desk and laptop ready to go for when I started writing my sermons. Two more doors on each side of the office, the master bedroom and, on the other side, a second bedroom. I threw my bag on the bed, got changed in more comfortable clothes, and lay on the couch, with a blanket and a fire going.

*This could have been a huge milestone for us,* I thought to myself. Truth be told, taking a job so far from my home wasn't just a way to jump-start my career and ministry; it was a way to escape. I was heartbroken. She was gone, and even after all this, I still couldn't get over everything that happened. I wanted to be with her again, but I couldn't get her back. Some nights I lay in bed and couldn't help but think of all the what-ifs and things that I would change if I could have to begin with. Overall, I was a happy guy, and I'd like to think I was fun to be around. But some nights, especially nights when something big happened, like getting the new job or the move, I couldn't help but think about how much better this would be if she were by my side to celebrate with me. I'd been on a few dates since she left me and even had a couple of serious relationships, but every time I looked back on my past love life, all I could see was her. I remembered my mother telling me, in life you have three loves. Your first love, if it ends, will always be the most painful. You've never experienced heartbreak, so it's hard to get over. Your second love, if it ends, is less painful, but it takes longer to get over. You start to reflect on things you've done wrong and how you can improve. You can have several "second loves" until you figure out what you want in life, then when it finally clicks, you'll meet your third love and things will work out. Lucy was my second love but everything I wanted in my third. I just couldn't wrap my mind around everything that happened all these years later. I lay on the couch, covered in my blanket, listening to the fire crackle. I started to say a prayer but slowly fell asleep. Sleep finally found me.

I'm twenty-four years old right now. Between everything I've been through and the places I've been, it's a miracle from God that I'm even alive. Back in 2017, when I was still a teenager and not even out of high school yet, I was bulimic. *Bulimia nervosa* is defined as an eating disorder where someone will eat large portions of food and then use methods to burn the calories off. That includes forcing yourself to vomit, over-exercising, taking laxatives. Bulimia and eating disorders messed up the early part of my life. Just like any addict, though, I did my best to hide it from others, but just like most addicts, too, I failed at doing it. At my worst, I was six foot five and 130 pounds.

## October 2017

I grew up in the small town of Leesburg, New Jersey. It was a very quiet, farm-like town where everyone knew one another and, for the most part, got along. We had a post office, a pizzeria, a church, and a graveyard all in the same block. Besides that, just houses, woods, and open fields and a few loading docks that took you out to the bay. There was also a small corner store, but if you wanted to go somewhere big like a mall or Walmart, you had to go to the next town over in Millville, which was also where I (along with all the other kids from Leesburg) went to school. I lived with my parents, Michelle and Randall Steele. I was the youngest of two. My older sister, Emily, was married and had moved out. She lived in Millville with her husband, Blake, who worked at the prison. Emily worked as a paramedic.

While my mother was a nurse aide, and my dad worked at the prison as well; most males in Leesburg did. My dad and I didn't get along very well. I was an unplanned child, unlike my sister, so he was emotionally distant from me most of the time. He drank a lot too. He and I would get into arguments, and he told me all the time that he didn't care if I was around or not. I never fully understood what I did to him, but he'd tell me all the time that if it weren't for my mom, I wouldn't be here. I didn't understand how a dad could treat his kid like that, so I spent most of my time at home, either with my mom or my room.

I was seventeen and a junior in high school at that time, with nothing to worry about. I had a good head on my shoulders. Though I didn't know what I fully wanted to do when I graduated high school, I had an idea of maybe law enforcement or military. I had a great GPA and was the tallest person in the high school choir, where I spent most of my days after school. My buddy Brandon and I would go up to the choir room most days and hang out with the choir director for an hour, waiting for my shift to start at work. I worked after school, but instead of driving twenty minutes back home, I just waited at the school. I had my truck then, but I usually didn't drive it to school to save money on gas; I only drove to school on days I had work after. Being a high school student who only worked part-time, I didn't make too much money. Especially since the minimum wage was 8.50. But every four days, I would go down to the beach, if it wasn't raining. It was a forty-minute drive, but when I got there, I would walk down to the jetty and sit and have food. I am obsessed with the ocean and watching the tide come in and out. Overall, from the outside, my life was perfect.

The only thing that happened was a heartbreak. This was my first love, the first girl I ever dated. Her name was Shelly. We dated over the summer and broke off at the very end of it. Summer love is a beautiful thing. So is young love. But being in love during the summer while you're young, that together is worth living for, those are two of the sweetest types there is. Together, though, was an amazing experience. You hear about young love in the movies, you hear about it in songs, you hear about it in ads and even books, but no matter how perfect it sounds there, it seems to be that sweet in real life, especially after some get their heart broken. In this case, I was the one who got their heart broken.

Looking back on my past, I can see now that I was just a kid. When dealing with the eating disorder and the break-ups, it felt like I was grown, but really, I was just a teenager that was dealing with problems I couldn't fight alone. I just needed help and someone to talk to. It's taken me so long to come to this conclusion, but looking back, I can see things with a better lens.

# CHAPTER 1

I leaned back in the chair in the choir room to stretch my arms and legs. It was a rainy Tuesday, around noon. I had choir for my third class of the day, right before gym. Most days, the choir director would send the basses of the choir to a back room for us to practice on our own while he worked with the rest of the choir. That was where we were, the back room of the choir room, ignoring the music we should be practicing and acting and talking like most unsupervised teenage boys or young adults would, discussing dream cars, dream jobs, sports, and practically any girl that walked and had a pulse. Even though we were surrounded by girls in the choir most of the time, it was very rare that one of us ever got a date. The only one of us who could even hold a solid relationship back then was Brandon. He and his girlfriend were together for years, and we didn't see them breaking up anytime soon.

Brandon was one of my best friends back then, and he still is today. Through everything I went through, I could always count on him being there for me. Same for him—anything he went through, he knew that I would back him up no matter what. We went to school together for as long as I could remember. He was shorter than me, dark-brown hair that he kept short, and patchy facial hair that none of us could convince him to shave. Brandon and I hung out a lot with a guy named Tanner. He was just as tall as me, but more built. He played sports in high school, and he was probably the easiest guy to joke around with. Tanner was a big Philadelphia Eagles fan, and Brandon…well, besides his girlfriend, Lilly, his world revolved around the Dallas Cowboys. Brandon and Tanner would give each other a hard time all the time. In the choir room that day, they were doing just that.

"The Cowboys didn't do that horrible last season. I can actually see them going to the Superbowl in the next couple of years," Brandon said.

"Dude, you're a freaking idiot! They won't even make the playoffs," Tanner said.

"C'mon, bro, what are you? An Eagles fan? How many rings do they have?"

"You always pull that card. The Cowboys haven't been to the Superbowl since the nineties. You might as well take that argument to the history room, bro."

I was zoning out; I was trying my best to stay awake, and the Monster Energy Drink I had for lunch didn't do a thing in my favor. We went to choir right after lunch, and I could already feel the crash from the caffeine and sugar hitting me.

"Larry, what do you think?" Tanner asked.

"What?" I said, zoning back in. "I'm sorry, what was that?"

"He's in his own world," Brandon said.

"Cowboys probably ain't winning in that one either," Tanner said with a half-grin on his face. There was a moment of silence while Brandon tried to think of a good comeback.

"All right, you idiot, listen her—"

"Larry," Mr. Sean said. He poked his head into the room. "The guidance office called. They need to see you down there right now. I told them you were on your way."

I nodded at him and got up.

"Shouldn't the rest of you be practicing?" Mr. Sean said, looking at the other guys.

I walked down the hallway in my faded blue jeans and shiny brown leather cowboy boots. There was a big difference between the town I lived in and Millville, the city where we all went to school. In simple terms, country and rock definitely weren't played a lot in Millville, and I didn't fit in as well as most people did in Millville schools. Comparing Millville to Leesburg was like comparing Texas to New York City when it came to city versus country. When I got to the guidance office, I stood in the doorframe and knocked on the door.

"Hey!" Mr. Pratt said, getting out of his chair. "C'mon in, Larry. Have yourself a seat." He extended his hand, and I shook it and sat down. In front of the desk. He and the guidance counselor Mrs. Bacon were sitting across from me.

"Would you like a water?" he asked.

"No. Thank you, though," I said. As I was talking, another guidance counselor came in and sat in the back of the room.

"Hello, Larry," she said, sitting down. I turned around and said hello back to her. Then she got up and sat down in the chair next to me. I turned back and faced Mr. Pratt and Mrs. Bacon.

"I got to say, two guidance counselors and a principal in the same room doesn't look good," I said. "Is there something I did wrong?"

"Oh no. No, no," Mr. Pratt said. "It's not that at all. We…um, needed to call you down to go over a couple of things with you. We want you to know, though, that this is nothing you did."

"Well, what is it?" I asked.

Mr. Pratt nodded at Mrs. Bacon.

"Larry," she said and paused. "We just got off the phone with your sister. There has been an accident involving your mother." There was a brief moment of silence.

"What kind of accident?" I said, sitting up in the chair. I could feel myself tensing up.

"We don't know every detail," she said. "According to your sister, she was heading to her boss's office after her break. Someone ran a red light while she was going through a major intersection."

"Is she okay?" I asked.

"Larry," Mrs. Bacon said. The other guidance counselor put her hand on my shoulder. "The paramedics who arrived on the scene did the absolute best they could do."

"What are you saying?" I asked. Tears started flooding my eyes. Even though they didn't say it yet, I already knew.

"She didn't make it, Larry. I'm very sorry. I know there's no easy way to say this," Mrs. Bacon said. The other guidance counselor moved in a little closer to me. Despite everything that was happening and how I felt, I could tell she was trying to be sincere.

"We are here for you—"

"This isn't happening," I said. "You're lying."

"Denial is the first stage of grieving," the woman next to me said. "I know this is har—"

"Don't pull that social-work bull with me!" I yelled. At this point, tears were pouring out of my eyes. I stood up, turned, and put my hands on the wall. My whole world right there just stopped on a dime. I didn't know what to say. I just stood there, holding in every tear I could; a few of them slipped through, though. Mr. Pratt stood up and approached me.

"I'm really sorry, son," he said. "Look, I'm not a guidance counselor anymore, but I was at one point. If you ever need to talk, man-to-man. We couldn't get in touch with your dad, but your sister is on her way to pick you up. I'll have someone from your class bring your stuff down. I want you to take the rest of the week off school. They're excused."

I nodded and pulled myself together the best I could. He patted me on the back, and we left the room and walked down to his office. I sat in silence, waiting for my sister to arrive.

When Emily got to the school, we threw our arms around each other. She stood there and cried while I hugged her, and I did my best to hold it all in. I couldn't cry, not in public, definitely not in front of my sister. It took every part of me, but I kept it all inside. The drive home was quiet for the most part. We turned the radio on low and let the music distract us. I don't know if it was from the crashing of the energy drink or holding all my tears in, but I was slowly starting to doze off.

"Does Dad know?" I finally asked and broke the silence; my voice was cracking from my holding in my tears.

"Yeah. He's her emergency contact," she replied in a voice very low and soft as silk. "The hospital called him out of work. He's probably home right now."

The rest of the drive was quiet. I didn't know what to say or how to say it. At this point, I couldn't even think about holding a conversation.

When I got home, my dad wasn't. Assuming he went back to work, I went into the kitchen and sat down at the table. The time on the oven said it was 1:30 p.m. I sat down and buried my face in my hands and finally let it out. Tears poured down my face and continued to do so. I was tired, crashing. Crying always makes you tired too, so I got even more exhausted. I covered my face the best I could with my arms and yelled into them. I started to beat the table until my hand started to hurt; the remaining emotions, I just bottled up. *Try to calm down,* I told myself. I walked out to the living room and lay down on the couch. I looked back at the time; it was 2:00 p.m. I lay back and closed my eyes. "Please, God, help me," I whispered and fell asleep almost immediately.

# CHAPTER 2

I woke up to the sound of the door slamming shut loud. It scared me, and I sat up almost instantly to see my dad walking through the living room into the kitchen. I got up and followed him into the kitchen and looked at the time again: 2:20 a.m. I stood in the doorframe while he rummaged through the refrigerator.

"Hey, Dad," I said. My dad turned his head and looked at me and ignored me and went back into the fridge. "How are you feeling?"

"Fantastic," he said, slamming lunch meat from the fridge on the kitchen table. "Fantastic! How about y-you? You came from school early, right?"

"Uh, yeah? Are you okay?"

"I said I was fine!" He shouted. I could smell his breath at this point.

"Are you drunk?" I asked.

He started making a sandwich again and ignoring the fact that I was there. I just sat there, watching him. It looked like he was going to pass out on himself. His hands were shaking, and his hair was a mess. He threw a sandwich together and sat at the kitchen table with that and another beer. He cracked open his beer and looked at me.

"What can I say?" he asked. "It should have been you." He took a sip out of his beer.

"Excuse me?" I said.

"I lost my wife today," he said in a soft voice, then he slowly started to get louder as he talked. "She's gone, and yeah, I'm drunk. But who cares at this point? It should have been you that died, not her."

"How can you even say tha—"

"Just shut up!" He started to raise his voice. "I just lost my wife today, and now I'm stuck with you. God took the wrong family member of mine. It should have been you, you stupid mistake!"

"I'm a mistake?" I yelled back at him.

"Yes, you are!" he yelled back. "Now that your mom is gone and I'm drunk, I'm free to speak my mind. You're a stupid mistake!"

"Really? Who do you think you are?" I yelled back at him.

"Watch your tone with me, boy." He stood up from his chair. "Like this is some big surprise? You knew I never wanted you here. Please, the only reason you stayed in this house is your mother."

"Like you're worth anything?" I asked. "What did you ever accomplish besides not drinking yourself to death before Mom died?" He backhanded me, and I fell against the wall. I got up and turned and punched him across the face. He grunted, then he returned and punched me in my gut. I tried my best to block it, but I couldn't, and I fell to my knees. It took me a couple of seconds to catch my breath.

"Get out of my house!" he yelled down at me while I was still on my knees, my hands covering my stomach from where he punched me. "I don't care where you go. But you better get out of here for the night before I hit you again. I don't care what happens with you at this point."

I got off my knees and stood there in silence as a tear ran down my face.

"Go!" he yelled. "Let's get moving!"

I walked out of the kitchen and up to my room.

"Your mother's not here to save you from the real world!" he yelled.

As I got to my room, a million thoughts raced through my head. *I can't believe this.* Tears poured down my face like a stream as I threw clothes into a gym bag and grabbed the keys to my truck. I didn't have much on me. I had the keys to my truck, a bag full of clothes, and a few pictures I put into my schoolbag. *Everything important,* I thought. I could hardly think at all at this point. I ran back down to the living room to see my dad sitting in his chair.

"I may be a drunk," he said as I walked past him, "but I'm more than you are, more of a man than you'll ever possibly be." I stood in the doorframe of the house. I turned and looked at him. He was in pretty good shape besides a little gut. Stubby beard and dark black hair slowly starting to gray. He was taller than me, and I don't know how much hate could be in one man. To this day, I couldn't understand it.

"Well, you set the bar so low it won't take much for me to get better."

"Just get out," he said, chuckling. *Law & Order: Special Victims Unit* was on the TV. My dad my entire life did nothing but come home after work, drink beer, and sit in his chair and watch that show. He watched *Law & Order*, *Charmed*, whatever came on TNT that night. If his show wasn't recorded from earlier, he'd make everyone in the house know about it.

"I love you, Dad."

He sat in silence, watching the TV.

"That's okay. I love you, anyway. Mom did too."

"You thought I was bluffing when I said your mom is the only reason you're still here, didn't you?" he asked. I turned briefly to look at him but bit my tongue and walked out without saying anything.

I walked out of the house to be greeted by the cold air. It was really cold. I got in my truck and started driving to my sister's house. Like I said, something is relaxing about driving in the middle of the night. The cold, the heat beating your face and windshield, and whatever song on the radio you wanted to play.

When I got to Emily's house, I grabbed my beat-up bag and walked to and knocked on Emily's door. I could hear her dog barking and scratching at the front door. Blake opened the door in his blue robe. I greeted his tired and confused face with a fake grin and a forced chuckle.

"Hey!" I said in a cracked voice. I was still trying to hold in tears. Blake started rubbing his eyes. He looked confused and probably thought he was dreaming. Their dog calmed down when she saw it was just me.

"Larry?" he said and coughed a little. His voice was soft and scratchy from just waking up. "What are you doing here?"

"It's kind of a funny story," I said and stared at him. After a brief pause in my voice, I continued. When bad things happen, humans always say it's kind of a funny story when, truth be told, there's not a funny thing about it. "Dad threw me out, and I don't have anywhere to go."

"Geez." He shook his head. "It's freezing out here. Come inside." He stepped aside and allowed me to walk in. Emily was standing at the bottom of the stairs.

"Dad threw me out," I said, looking at her. She stood there and was quiet for a couple of seconds. I woke her up too, so she was trying to fully wake up and process what I said. When she finally understood what I was saying, she threw her arms around me. I continued to hold every tear I could in. *Bottle it up, bottle it up, bottle it up,* I kept thinking.

"I'm sorry," she said. "I suspected he would, though I didn't think he actually would. You're welcome to stay with us while things with him get sorted out."

"If they ever do," I added and lifted my shirt, showing the bruise his fist left when he punched my stomach. "To be honest, I kind of hit him too." Emily looked shocked at both the bruise and what I told her.

"Oh my goodness, Larry!" Emily yelled, covering her mouth. "Look, you can just stay here for now. If things are that bad, I don't want you going back there alone."

I nodded, and she hugged me again.

"Do you need anything?" Blake asked. "Water? Coffee?"

"No," I said. "I'm sorry, can we talk about this in the morning? I'm awfully tired."

"I got to be up for work in a few hours," Blake said, smiling. Then he chuckled. "That's fine with me. I'll take you to the guest room."

I grabbed my bag, and we walked down the hallway next to the stairs. The last room at the end of the hallway was a guest room. When we opened the doors and turned the lights on, I saw a usual-size room. A full-size bed, a dresser, and a nightstand next to the bed with a Bible on it. Blake was a pastor's kid, so he was always a devoted Christian himself.

"Are you going to be okay?" he asked. "I don't mind missing a couple of hours of sleep if you need to talk."

"I'm fine," I said, I was lying but I didn't want to keep him up. I just said I was fine and tried to pull off the lie by nodding my head. Blake patted me on the back.

"Get some sleep, bud." He walked away and I closed the door and threw my bag on the floor and threw myself onto the bed. In one day, just one day, almost everything I knew changed. My mom, my dad, where I was living. I laid in bed and tears flooded over my eyes. This wouldn't be the last time I cried myself to sleep. It was the first of many. I turned my head and looked at the Bible that was sitting on the nightstand. *There can't be a god,* I told myself. I picked up the Bible and put it into the drawer of the dresser, where I couldn't see it. With that, I closed my eyes, and sleep finally found me.

Suddenly, I was dreaming that I was a kid again. I was running on the beach with my parents. I was in middle school. I always went running because I had dreams of running track when I got to high school. It was just me and the wind running up the beach to meet the jetty while my parents fell behind because they were walking. I was in much better shape back then. I played basketball with my friends, and I went running almost every day or at least went for a bike ride. It was more simple times back then. My dad had a drinking problem then, too, but at least we were on "okay" terms when he was sober then. In my dream I was running. I was right about to get to the jetty when storm clouds rolled in, and my mom started yelling for me. "Larry!" she yelled for me. But I kept running. "Larry!" she kept yelling at me. I went a little farther when it started to storm heavily. I started to get scared. One more time my mom yelled, "Larry!" I woke up and sat up and screamed. I was breathing heavily. I was sweating really bad. Everything was okay somewhat. I lay back down and tried to sleep. This was the first night terror I ever had; I knew the sweat was from stress. It took me a while to get my heart rate back to normal. I closed my eyes, hoping this would all go away. I finally fell back to sleep again.

I woke up in a dark room. My phone said it was nine in the morning. I could have sworn that last night was all just a dream—even worse, a nightmare. It wasn't. Emily and Blake weren't home. I lay in bed for a few minutes to look at my phone. My Facebook timeline and phone were filled with messages and posts of people telling me how sorry they were for my loss. People I hadn't even heard from in months, and even years. Maybe it was that I still felt sleepy, or I was still trying to understand and cope with everything that happened yesterday, but the messages and posts felt no different from someone wishing you a happy birthday on Facebook, or a merry Christmas. People just say it to say it, and just like that, you don't hear from them until the next year. Nevertheless, I messaged everyone back and thanked them for thinking about me and rolled myself out of bed and opened the bedroom curtains. I didn't tell anyone about what happened with my dad; it was none of their business. I still didn't even fully understand or grasp what was happening.

*I'm going to have to go back to Dad's house and get my things,* I thought. But I didn't let that bother me. I hadn't felt this low and down in a while, and I couldn't let my dad bring me down any further. I sat in the living room and started to doze off while the coffee was brewing. I slept a lot, but I still felt tired from the night before. I could feel my stomach and the bruise. I was hurting from it.

My phone rang.

"Hello?"

"Larry." It was Brandon. "I wanted to talk to you in school, but you're not here. I don't blame you. How are you feeling?"

"Not too good," I said. My voice was still scratchy. Yelling the night before when I woke up sure didn't help me any.

"I'm so sorry about your mom," he said. "She was a sweet woman. It broke my heart, too, when I heard the news. You know, we're here for you during all this. Anything you need, just let us know."

"Thanks, bro."

"Look, I can't talk on the phone long. I gotta get to class. But I just needed to check in on you. You know, what normally cheers me up is doing something that would make me happy. Go for a jog, watch something on Netflix. I know you're always disappearing to that jetty on the beach. Maybe go there?"

I just nodded in agreement, like he could tell I was doing anything over the phone.

"They gave me the rest of the week off school," I said.

"Okay, good!" he said. "Hey, I'm having a little party at the end of the week for Halloween. Nothing much, but we are having a get-together, and I want you to go."

"I'm guessing I'm not getting out of it," I said with a fake chuckle.

"*You* guessed right, my man," he said. "Look, I gotta go, though. Try to do something that you enjoy. Don't just lie around. It'll only make you feel worse."

With that, he hung up. Maybe he was right, though. Maybe I did need to get out of the house.

I went back into the kitchen and drank my coffee while playing some games filled with ads on my phone and walked outside to meet the day. I started with a walk. Since I was now living at my sister's house, I went for a walk to get used to the surrounding neighborhood. It was a normal suburban neighborhood. Everyone seemed to be friendly to one another (surprisingly for New Jersey). What started as a walk turned into a jog, however, and even a little bit of running. Maybe exercise was what I needed. I ran for a good thirty minutes before getting back into my sister's house. Now, I wasn't unhealthy, but I definitely wasn't in the best shape of my life, so when I got inside, I was sweating like a pig and, honestly, felt like death. I ran inside and chugged water super quickly and ripped my shirt off, going into the bathroom, with anticipation of getting a shower. Before the bathroom sink was a scale.

I was six foot two. I wasn't fat, but I had some meat to me. Between my jog and the way I felt, maybe I could stand to lose a couple of pounds. In middle school, I was in much better shape. No matter what, I always had running and basketball to lean on. So maybe exercising and working out could be a good way to cope during all this. Maybe I should set a goal to get in as good a shape as I was in middle school. Even though things seemed bad, keeping my body in good shape could be something I could control right now. So I stepped on the scale to see what my current weight was, so I'd have something to go off: 202 pounds.

*Not bad,* I thought. *You can definitely start losing weight, though. You can handle this.*

Less than twenty-four hours ago, I found out I lost my mom. Less than eighteen hours ago, my dad told me I was scum to him and kicked me out. Everything in my life felt like it was out of my control and it was out of my reach; maybe this could be the one thing I could control. But the excitement of thinking about getting in good shape was leaving me, the emotional hurt settling back in. I turned the shower on and got up and sat down in the shower and let the hot water run over me. I buried my head into my hands, and I cried again.

I stayed home most of the day. Besides my run, I just lay in bed and watched whatever I could find interesting on Netflix. I kept my lunch and dinner small, too, so my run didn't feel like my job was for nothing. Emily got home and I talked with her too, but mainly I just kept quiet, isolated in my new room at her house, while sending thank-you texts back to people who sent me messages on Facebook, even people I hardly even talked to anymore. That was what I did for the next few days until I went to Brandon's house that Friday. I just went on runs, watched Netflix, and ate a couple of times a day. I still felt horrible, but I felt comfort in going on runs. It boosted the confidence I had in myself, like a new way to feel accomplished. By the time Friday rolled around, I even found a way to make myself laugh at some of the things I saw on movies and memes on Facebook. I was starting to feel somewhat better; it was only week 1, though.

    That evening, right before the sun started to go down, I went to my dad's house to collect the rest of my belongings. I knew he'd be at work, so I went when I didn't have to confront him. Blake took me to help carry things out. I didn't have much besides DVDs, video games, and music collection. It was little, but it was things I cared about. The moment I stepped into the living room, the smell of beer hit me.

    "Pew," Blake said; he could smell it too. The second we went upstairs, we collected all my belongings as quickly as possible and rushed downstairs. I went back into the house.

    "Stay here, Blake," I said. "I'll only be a second."

    I stepped back into the house to look around. My entire life thus far, my entire childhood, was spent in this house. I remembered learning how to read and write here. I remembered the dog I got as a kid that passed the year before. I felt like I was in the movie *Dream House*. Daniel Craig played an author who thought his entire life was coming together when he left his job to be with his wife and kids, but it fell apart. On the wall was a picture of the entire family. My parents, my sister, and me. I looked toward it, that perfect family in the picture. That perfect, happy little family. The correctional officer and nurse aide that fell in love and had two children. The perfect family that always stuck together. Things always seemed perfect, but they weren't. Suddenly, I was wondering if something that perfect could even exist.

I walked back outside to meet Blake at his car.

"Everything okay?" he asked. I was getting into the passenger seat quietly. I was doing my best to hold in tears, but my face was turning red. I started scratching the side of my head.

"Hey, it's all okay, man. I can fully understand if you don't want to talk about it. If I were you, I wouldn't want to talk about it either. Let's just listen to music on the way back home."

"Okay," I forced myself to say without any tears coming out.

"Also, I know it might be easier to talk to me about these things rather than your sister. I know how emotional she can be at times." He started laughing, and I put on a fake smile. "Just know, I know sometimes talking to a man can be easier. Whenever you're comfortable, you can talk to me about these things. Whatever you do, please don't bottle this up. If not me, talk to your friends, the guidance office, anything. All right? It doesn't have to be now, but later." He started nodding.

"All right," I said in a quiet voice. I was looking down at my lap. This was going to be a big transition. Blake turned on his radio, and K-Love was playing. A Christian music station. At this point, my faith had started to crumble. Even though

I wasn't a practicing Christian, I still thought God was real. It wasn't until this week that I was really questioning that. Of course, Blake, being a pastor's kid, was a Christian, so I didn't want to tell him my faith went away. I just listened to music on the way back. I quickly looked at my phone and sent a few messages back to more people telling me that they were sorry for my loss. Not one text from my dad; I didn't expect one, but I was hoping he'd message me when he sobered up. False hope, I guess. I stayed quiet for the entire ride home. I was wanting to get back and go to bed early.

# CHAPTER 3

I woke up Friday morning and stepped on the scale. Then the scale read 198 pounds. A smile hit my face for the first time in a week. Four pounds isn't a lot of weight, but it had only been a few days. I felt proud of myself for getting that accomplished. I went for my run, came home, and ate decent-size breakfast, more than what I ate the last few days. *I deserve this.*

My phone rang. It was Brandon.

"Hey!" I said into the phone.

"You sound happy," Brandon said. "I wanted to call to see if you were still coming over tonight?"

"Yeah, man, what time?"

"It starts at eight. I was wondering if you wanted to come over around six, though. There's food at the party, but I got some burgers I was fixin' to make. Maybe you and I can throw some down and play Xbox for a little with Tanner, if you're up to it?"

"I'm up for it," I said. "I'll see you in a bit, bro."

"Awesome, man!" he replied. "I'll see you there."

I put my phone down, ran and got into bed, and started to relax. The more I sat still, though, the more negative thoughts crept back into my mind. At this point, I still couldn't get over my mom. I missed her like crazy. I didn't want to think about Dad, but I knew I'd have to see him again at some point. The thought of that drove me crazy. I started to tear up. Wouldn't anyone?

*****

"Hey, bro!" Brandon yelled as he ran over and threw his arms around me. "I'm so glad you're here, man." He started patting me on the back.

"I am too," I said.

"I'm telling you, bro," he said, "tonight is going to be great for you. I got a feeling about this one." He ran over to the kitchen, and I followed him. He pulled out a couple of plates with heavy burgers on them. A load of fries and a two-liter bottle of Coke.

"All right, bro, help me bring these down to the basement. Tanner will be here in a few minutes. You and I can kill these."

Brandon had a house similar to my dad's; it was a huge living room with a kitchen and dining room connected to it. On the far side of the living room, there was a stairwell that led down to the basement that Brandon turned into a man cave. His parents traveled a lot for their work, so he got the house to himself most of the time. Good for him, because if anyone wanted to throw a party of some sort, it was always done at his house. We sat in his basement, eating, watching *The Office*, waiting for Tanner to show up to play the Xbox.

"I want to introduce you to someone tonight," he said.

"Who?" I asked, pushing fries into my mouth.

"My girlfriend, Lilly, she has a friend named Anna," he said. "Lilly and I agree that you two might get along. Considering the type of week you've had, it might not be as bad to meet someone who could help take your mind off things."

Truth be told, he was right—not to mention I still hadn't told him, or anyone besides my sister and Blake, about what happened with my dad. I didn't want him to continue to feel bad for me on top of feeling bad because of my mom. My mind went to focus on eating. I had had a large breakfast, lunch, and now I was eating a huge dinner, not to mention that I'd be eating pizza and snacks at the party. Also, I'd possibly be drinking. I was getting nervous that I was putting back on the weight I was losing. I had worked hard all week, and for some reason, the thought of not being able to control my weight the way I wanted to was making me upset. I started to feel fat and ashamed.

"What's going on, folks?" Tanner yelled, coming down the stairs.

"My man!" Brandon yelled.

*Try to focus on Tanner,* I thought. But the more I tried to focus, the more nervous I got. I worked hard this week to drop my weight down to what I had it at. I couldn't just lose an entire week in one night; controlling my weight was the best thing I had now. It wasn't a horrible feeling, but the full feeling I got from eating all this food started to make me feel uncomfortable.

"You feeling okay?" Tanner asked.

"What?" I asked. "Oh yeah, I'm okay," I said.

"I'm sorry to hear about your mom, man," Tanner said. "I brought a case of Bud Light I sneaked out of my dad's garage for the party. I want you to try to have a good time tonight," he said.

"Definitely," I said. "Excuse me, I need to go to the bathroom."

I ran back upstairs. I ran into the bathroom and shut the door as quickly as I could and looked myself in the mirror. *It's okay, it's okay, it's okay,* I tried telling myself. But the thought of not being able to control my weight right now was bothering me. I didn't know what to do. I started to think. People who want to stay skinny do all types of things to lose weight; I just had to calm down. *This isn't the end of the world,* I thought to myself, and finally, I knew what I wanted to do. I lifted the toilet bowl and fell to my knees before it, and I started to force the food I just ate back up. From where I hadn't eaten too much all week, it was very easy. A slight burp made food come back up after all the food I just ate. I'd never done something like this before, making myself vomit. My eyes started watering, and I could feel pressure in the front of my face.

The vomit coming up made my throat burn a little. The act of doing this made my heart feel like it was bursting into a million pieces. It was a little painful, and overall, it made me feel uncomfortable. I purged and tried to purge for a good five minutes, until all that was left was gagging and nothing coming up. I turned and sat down on the bathroom floor and hugged my knees and rested my chin on my knees. Snot ran down my face, and I could feel tears rolling down with it. I missed being home with my parents. Even if he didn't care what was going on with me right now, I missed my dad. I definitely missed my mom. Everything in my life just felt totally messed up. *It's okay, it's okay,* I told myself again. This time, though, I started to believe myself. I wiped the snot and tears from my face with toilet paper and flushed the toilet. I didn't know what I just did to myself, but what I ate was gone and I felt satisfied. All the stress and tension that I was feeling just ten minutes ago was gone, and I could relax for the rest of the night.

"There he is!" Brandon said as I was walking downstairs. "You feeling okay? You were up there a while."

"Yeah," I said. "A lot better."

"How about we crack open the case?" he asked.

"That sounds good," I said.

For a party "being nothing special," I would have loved to see what a big party would be like. His basement was packed full of people from high school, and there was plenty of music and food. Of course, since we were high schoolers, we kept the alcohol part the best secret we could, but everyone was drinking. There was loud music, and everyone was having a good time. Brandon made a rule that if you brought something to smoke, including Juul, you had to do it out back. Me, I found a corner of the basement and had a seat with my drink. I hummed to the music playing but overall tried to keep to myself. The thought of vomiting earlier was on my mind a lot. It made me feel relieved. But deep down, I knew that it shouldn't. I felt guilty about it, but it relaxed me. *I can't do that again,* I told myself. *That's not normal. It can't be healthy. Not again.*

"Larry! My man!" Brandon flopped down in the chair next to me and put his arms around my shoulder. "You feeling okay?"

"I don't know, man," I said. "I feel good, really good, actually. I don't think I'm supposed to, though. So I want to feel happy, but I feel guilty if I do. What do you do with that?" Of course, I left out the reason I felt good was that I made myself vomit.

"You have fun with your bro," he said jokingly. Then he got serious. "I know it's hard, but let me tell you, things get better. As time goes on, it will hurt less. I'm not saying it goes away fully, but you'll learn to live with it." He smiled at me.

"My dad threw me out," I said.

"What?" he said.

I explained to him everything. From my dad throwing me out, to the fact that I had moved in to my sister's house. He seemed mad that I didn't tell him right away, but he understood that it's not something you are excited to talk about. But we continued to talk and sip on beer during the party. I still couldn't tell him about what I did earlier. It was only a onetime thing. I couldn't make him worry any more about me than he already did. *It was only an onetime thing, nothing else,* I continued to tell myself. *I shouldn't tell anyone about it.*

"I know what will cheer you up," he said. "That girl Lilly invited to the party, she's standing over there across the room. Go talk to her. Get your mind straight."

"I don't know, ma—"

"Young man!" he yelled, standing up. "Get over there and talk to her, or so hel—"

"Okay, Dad," I said, chuckling and standing with him. He patted me on the back, and I started walking toward her. It had been a while since I talked to a girl. I hadn't even talked to girls much since I and Shelly broke things off. I stood about six feet behind her, not knowing what to say as she was talking to her friends. Heart pounding, getting nervous, I stood there for about a minute, trying to figure out what to say and if I had a plan.

"Larry, you klutz!" I heard Brandon yelled, and he pushed me forward and I fell into her, spilling my beer all over the back of her shirt and falling to the ground. The girl fell forward, but her friends prevented her from falling over. I lay on my back with my eyes shut. I hit my arm on the ground and hurt it. I was fine; there would at least be some bruising from it, though. I opened my eyes.

"What was that?" I asked myself, looking up. She and Lilly were looking down at me. I got beer all over my shirt, her shirt, and the floor.

"Larry!" Brandon said, pulling me to my feet. "You have to watch where you're going! Are you two okay?"

"No, you got beer all over me!" she yelled. "I can't go home like this. My parents will kill me!"

"I'm so sorry," I said, grabbing my arm, with it still being sore. "I have a T-shirt in my car, if you need one? Brandon can wash yours in the meantime?"

"Sure, I can do that. You two better get going!" Brandon replied with a big grin on his face. He leaned into me. "You're welcome."

"Whatever. I'm getting you back for that shove," I said.

"Even with a wingman you still fell. That was kind of hilarious." Brandon grabbed Lilly and pulled her away. I'm not sure what he thought a wingman does, but I'm pretty sure a wingman does anything but that.

"My truck is this way," I said, and we walked toward the stairs, mostly in silence. When we got to my truck, I pulled a shirt out of my bag, which I never unpacked when I moved in with my sister. She quickly ran back inside and changed and threw some of Brandon's mom's perfume on to try her best to cover up the beer smell. She looked beautiful. She was thinner and taller, about five foot nine. She had long dark-red hair that hung down just below her shoulders. There were some freckles around her face. Overall, she was absolutely beautiful. I knew when she came back out that I would have to say something to her. When we finally came out, she looked at me and gave me a sarcastic smile. *Say something! Say something!* I started thinking to myself. *Think!*

"I'm Larry, Larry Steele."

"I'm Anna Jones," she said back. "Out of curiosity, you don't think I'm really that dumb to believe that stunt you and Brandon did was actually real, do you?"

"You mean you don't believe that I actually fell into you somehow after my idiot friend told me to be careful and pushed me? I wouldn't believe that either. I mean, the least he could have done was push me then tell me to be careful."

She started laughing a little.

"Yeah, and there's also the fact Lilly told me about you and that she was going to introduce us."

"I just wish we could have met on better terms," I said, laughing with her. She went from giving me a sarcastic smile to actually laughing. Not bad steps so far.

"Do you want to go for a walk while my shirt washes?" she asked. "It'll be better to talk in a not-so-loud environment."

"I'd like that," I said.

She went to make sure that her shirt was actually washing, and we went outside for a walk. I started to think about all this. Maybe talking to a new girl could help me feel better. Of course, with everything on my mind, it took forever to get past the small talk in the conversation. After we had fully talked and got to know each other a little better, she turned out to be a sweet and cool person. She loved movies and reading, she ran track for our high school, she had already been applying for colleges, and she told me she wasn't 100 percent certain on what she wanted to do but she had a strong feeling that she wanted to be a vet or do something with working for animals. She also had a higher-pitched, shy voice. It was adorable. Overall, she was one of the coolest girls that I had ever met so far.

The girl I dated before, she was a girl named Shelly. I met her at the church my mom used to take me to. Of course, I stopped going because of what happened to my mom. But

Shelly seemed nice when we started talking at first. I thought things were going good, but she just randomly said it was over and left. It broke my heart, and of course, a few months after that, everything with my parents went down. But something with Anna just seemed *different*. Even if it was only one night, I felt that we could have a strong connection. She pulled out her phone to text Lilly to make sure her shirt was in the dryer. That was a good sign to me. She wasn't in a rush to get back to the house.

"So, Larry," she said, "what's the plan after high school?"

"I have no idea," I said. Up until this point, I wanted to do law enforcement or military. I just didn't think I could follow in my dad's footsteps anymore, not after everything that happened. He did both the military and corrections after that. I couldn't tell her about this, though. Not now. I just met her; I couldn't tell her anything sad about my life. "I probably will start with a community college. See where it takes me from there."

"I can't believe I haven't seen you around the school before," she said.

"Well…" I paused for a moment and smiled at her. "I'm glad we met now."

"Me too," Anna said back to me, and she smiled.

We walked around the neighborhood for almost three hours. Just talking about our plans and goals in life. We played twenty questions and talked about our family. I told her I currently lived with my sister. I told her my mom died, but she already knew that from Lilly telling her earlier in the day. Of course, I left out the details about Dad. She amazed me. The more we talked, the more I thought to myself over again that this girl was amazing. When we finally got back to the house, she got her shirt out of the dryer and changed back into it. Almost everyone at the house was gone except

Lilly, Brandon. Also Tanner, who was still in the basement, hanging out with Brandon. Lilly was waiting for us in the house, and when she saw us, she ran.

"There you are. I was wondering when you were going to get back. Are you ready to go?" Lilly asked.

"Yeah," she said. "Uh, can you give us a minute?" Lilly looked frustrated but nodded.

"I'll be in the car," she said and walked off. She'd already given us hours; what were a few more minutes going to do?

"I had…," we both said at the same time, then stopped. Lilly smiled.

"I had a great time tonight," I said. "I'd like to see you again. Would you want to grab something to eat sometime? Or maybe go to a movie?"

"I'd really like that a lot," she told me. She gave me her phone and told me to put my number in it. When I did, she threw her arms around me. She gave me a big hug, and my heart started racing from it.

"Bye, Larry," she said and walked off to the car.

I walked down into the basement, and the second I got there, Tanner threw a handful of pretzels at me.

"There's the betrayer who skipped out on the party for some girl."

"Okay, well, you're clearly drunk. But let's save that conversation for another time," I said, laughing.

"Betrayer," Tanner said.

"Leave the betrayer alone. He was shooting his shot," Brandon said. "You better have secured her number, though, my dude."

"The dude shot, and he succeeded!" I yelled.

"My man!" Tanner said, laughing. "It's about freaking time you got another date." Tanner was sitting backward on a recliner; he threw his arms and head over the back of it and was looking at us.

"Well?" Brandon asked. "How was she? Lilly and I have been trying to get you two together ever since your last relationship ended. We just never figured out the right time to introduce y'all. We thought tonight's party would be a better time than any."

Brandon and Lilly had been together for longer than any other high school relationship I'd seen. I'd known Brandon since elementary school, and he started dating Lilly when we were in eighth grade. For only being seniors, they did a good job of acting like my parents. Introducing me to different girls, downing some of the clothes I wore. Tanner, the rest of the group, and I made fun of them for it and called them Mom and Dad when they did it. It had gotten to the point that they didn't even realize they did it. All Brandon was really missing were the corny jokes that made everyone cringe and question what comedy really was.

I told him everything. From the things we talked about to how long we talked. It honestly made me forget all about the things that had been going on in my life. I felt happier. It felt like a George Strait song. A boy meets a girl, the boy starts having feelings for the girl, and maybe if things go right, she'll like him back. But it's too close to tell. It was only my first night meeting her.

"I feel like I have butterflies in my stomach," I said.

"Same, bro," Tanner said. "That's probably from drinking too much, though."

"You be quiet," Brandon said, chuckling. "But speaking of stomachs, are you feeling okay?"

"Yeah, I'm fine. Why?"

"Well, I went to use the bathroom upstairs earlier in the night, and there was some vomit floating around in the toilet. It looked like the food we ate before the party. I just wanted to make sure you're not sick?"

My heart started pounding. *He knew,* I thought. My heart started pounding more, and I could feel my face starting to burn. *He can't know about this. He can't know about this.* I knew it couldn't have been healthy. I knew it definitely wasn't healthy, but for a friend to know what I just did would be embarrassing. He wouldn't have understood, anyway. I had to keep this to myself.

"Uh, yeah, I'm fine. I just got a little sick from eating too much. I ate a lot before I got here and shoved that food down as well. I just burped and some came up. I didn't mean to."

"Fatty," Tanner said.

"Shut it," I said while forcing a laugh to come up. "I'll see y'all later." Before I left, though, Brandon came up to me and threw his arms around me.

"Look, bro, I know you really needed tonight after all that happened. If you need anything else, just shoot me a text," he said.

"I will, bro," I said. "Thanks."

After that, I hurried out of the house. While leaving, I heard Tanner yell he was going to sleep in the guest room because we all knew he was in no shape to drive home tonight. I knew Tanner was drunk and just joking, but his calling me fat made me feel even worse about myself. But never mind that for now; I just gave a girl my number. Things seemed like they were going great. I also almost got caught forcing myself to vomit, which also made me scared on top of that. I ran out to my truck and got into it. I was breathing heavily. That was a close call. Too close. No one could know about this. Not my sister, not Brandon. No one. I had to keep this to myself. My mind shifted back to the night I had with Anna and how beautiful she looked. I had a text from her.

> *Hey, it's Anna. I had a fun night tonight. I'm looking forward to seeing you again. Night (:*

With that, I drove home and fell asleep.

## CHAPTER 4

I woke up in the morning to the sound of Miska barking and the smell of coffee brewing. I jumped out of bed and went to the bathroom and stepped on the scale to see if what I did yesterday changed anything: 194 pounds. A huge smile went across my face. *Holy crap!* I thought to myself. This was great! I made embarrassing hand gestures to show my excitement and went out to meet Emily and Blake sitting at the table, drinking coffee. I knew that my mom's funeral was coming up and that I'd have to miss it. It upset me more than I could express, but I couldn't see my dad. I didn't want to see him. So seeing the weight loss made me happier than I could have expressed.

"Morning!" I yelled, coming into the kitchen.

"Morning," Emily said. "You seem happy."

I spared details about last night, but I told her I met a girl. I left out the part about drinking and making myself vomit

"We're going out on a date soon, I hope!" I exclaimed.

"Congratulations, bud," Blake said.

We talked for another ten minutes before they got ready for work. The thought of what I did last night in the bathroom came across my mind. The thought of how much weight I lost, too, from doing it came across my mind. Maybe this wasn't as bad as I thought. I still couldn't let anyone know, but maybe it was not as big of a deal as I was making it. *Ah, 194 pounds,* I thought. That was really good. I went to go put my running clothes on, and I went for a run. Only this time, I went for a run that was a lot longer than the ones I normally went on. I was doing good. Just kept pushing myself.

When I came home, I went into the kitchen and made a cup of coffee. I thought about making breakfast. I had just gone for a good run, and breakfast is an important meal. I should eat. Then the thought of Anna came across my mind. I thought of the progress I had made so far. If I wanted to get down to my goal weight, I knew I had to make some sacrifices. I skipped breakfast. I chugged a cup of coffee and chased that down with a couple of bottles of water. It took away my hunger pangs. That was fine for now. *It'll be okay,* I thought. I went back to my room and climbed back into bed and fell asleep again.

## CHAPTER 5

Since Saturday, I was true to myself. I didn't make myself vomit anymore, but I did skip a few meals. The meals I did eat, I ate smaller portions of too. I hadn't been on the scale in a few days, but I knew I was making good progress in getting my weight down. My pants were a little more lose around my hips, and I had to start putting a belt on.

Right after school that day, Brandon and I sat up in the choir room with the director. Sean Hogan was his name. But since we were just about to graduate and we were closer to him than the other students, he let us call him Sean instead of Hogan or Mr. Hogan. He was tall, darker hair, and a five o'clock shadow. He was straight out of college too. Most girls in the choir seemed to have a puppy crush on him. A very opinionated man at that. He wasn't very Christian, or if he was, he just never talked about it. But he loved singing faith-based choir songs. He would say "it wasn't for the lyrics behind it but from the beautiful sound it had."

We sat in his office with him on days we had work after school. Work for me normally started an hour to two hours after school, and instead of driving all the way back to Leesburg, it was easier to hang at the school before going. He sat at his desk, looking at sheet music, while some sports station played low, Brandon sitting in a chair with his feet up, with a Monster Energy in front of him. And me? I sat by the window, wanting to text Anna, trying to think of the words to say.

"The Cowboys have been getting better over the past seasons since Prescott replaced Romo. We just need to work on a few things in our defense, but I can at least see us getting a playoff win," Brandon said.

"I don't see my Browns even making a win this year," Sean said, a little disappointed. From being from Cleveland originally, he was a Browns fan. Since the Browns didn't win often, Brandon loved talking about the Cowboys with him so Sean couldn't talk bad to him.

I lost track of what they were saying. I was sitting, facing them, but all my attention was focused on my phone. I wanted to text her, but I just saw her a few days ago. I didn't want to text too soon or late, but I wanted to say something. *Keep it simple,* I thought. I opened my phone and just texted, "Hey." Then I looked up and focused on Brandon and Sean again.

"You want the Browns to go to the Superbowl?" Brandon asked. "How about this: Later this week, we can all go to Taco Bell. I guarantee after that the Browns will be taken to the Superbowl." I put on a smile after hearing that, but I knew there was a reason I never listened to him when he went on about football.

My phone buzzed. She said: "Hey (: What are you up to?"

"I'm sitting in school, listening to Brandon rage about football."

We texted back and forth for a few minutes. I completely lost focus on Brandon and Sean; all my focus on that moment was on her. "Can I call you?" I asked. Without even texting back, she called me first.

"Excuse me, guys, I gotta go," I said. Before they could say anything back, I walked out of the room and answered the phone.

"Hey, what's up?" she asked.

I knew I wanted to ask her on a date, but I didn't want to do it through text. I didn't know when the next time I'd see her in person was either. I at least would have to do it over the phone. We talked for a few minutes before I got out of the school and to my truck.

"Are you busy this weekend?" I asked her.

"No, I'm not busy at all," she said.

"If you weren't, I was wondering if you'd maybe want to go out?" I said, and after a second paused, I added, "Like, on a date."

"I'd like that a lot," she said.

"Great!" I said "How's Friday night? I can pick you up around four thirty."

"That sounds nice," she said. "I'll see you then! I'll text you my address."

"I can't wait," I told her. "Bye."

At that moment, I literally jumped in joy and started fist-pumping the air. Excitement filled me, and I couldn't help but feel happy. I started patting my truck and giving a fake laugh.

My phone buzzed again. Thinking it was her, I got excited and looked at it, but it was Brandon. "Me and Sean can see your dumb ass. Stop dancing like an idiot and go to work." I looked up at the window on the second floor, where the choir room was, and saw them waving and laughing at me. I smiled and waved at them and went to work.

Later, when I got home, it was almost 9:00 p.m. Emily and Blake were already asleep. I walked in and tried my best to not wake the dog up, but she barked a couple of times and ran over to me. I got her to quiet down luckily before waking them up. There was a note on the counter.

> *I made dinner for us. Leftovers are in the fridge. Enjoy!*
>
> *Love,<br>Emily*

There was a pile of food in the fridge. Homemade pizza and pasta. I wanted to eat, but I couldn't. I wanted to stay in better shape, especially with the date coming up. But I had skipped several meals in the last few days already. My mind went back and forth as I stared at the food in the fridge. *I have to eat, I can't eat, but I need to.* My heart started pounding, and I started to feel anxiety. *Larry, this isn't you. This isn't you.* I couldn't resist anymore. I took all the leftovers out of the fridge, and I started eating it, all of it. I ate most of it down and chased it with a can of Coke that was in the fridge. It tasted good, and I felt good while I was doing it. *This is good,* I thought. I should be eating, anyway; I shouldn't be hurting myself. I continued to put the food down until my stomach felt so full I couldn't take in another bite.

I went into the living room and sat down on the recliner. It was dark and quiet. I sat there for a few minutes, thinking about what I just did. I sat and thought about all the food I ate. I started to feel guilty. *What did I just do?* I leaned forward in the chair, and my anxiety started to go through the roof. All I could think of was all the hard work I did in trying to lose weight just for me to eat all that food. I felt horrible. I felt disgusted with myself. Then I started to think of Anna. I wanted to look nice for her. She wouldn't like me anymore if I put too much weight on. I started sweating, and my hands started shaking.

I felt like any control I had was lost. I stood up and ran for the bathroom that was down the hall from my room and closed the door behind me. *One more time won't hurt me,* I thought. I bent over the toilet and started to vomit again for the second time. This time, the moment I started, I knew what I was doing was wrong, but I couldn't help feeling better as I was doing it. I felt disgusted with myself, but I felt better. I couldn't help but feel the anxiety and shame I felt moments ago get ripped away like a Band-Aid. When I was done, I stood up and wiped the vomit off my mouth with toilet paper and flushed the toilet and looked in the mirror. My face and eyes were red, snot hung out of my nose, and in my head I felt the pressure.

I felt ashamed again. I knew what I did was wrong. It felt good for a brief second, but I knew what I just did was wrong, and the shame came back. I threw cold water in my face, but this time, I remembered what happened at Brandon's house, so I made sure I flushed the toilet a second time. I went back to my room and crawled into bed. *Something is wrong with me,* I thought to myself. *Something is wrong with me, and I don't know what it is.* A million thoughts raced through my head as the shame and tears set in. I threw my head into the pillow and cried again. It wouldn't be the last time I cried myself to sleep in this bed.

# CHAPTER 6

"You look nice!" Emily said as I walked into the living room. It was Friday evening. I was all dressed and ready to take Anna out. I wore blue jeans, a blue flannel, and my hiking boots. I combed my hair and put my best cologne on.

"Where are you taking her?" Blake asked.

"There's a restaurant in Cape May," I said. "It's called Lobster House. It's pretty expensive, but I still have a gift card that I got, so it won't be too bad."

Emily came over and fixed the collar to my shirt, and then she hugged me.

"I know you've been going through a lot," Emily said. "I just want you to know that we are so proud of you. I want you to have fun tonight." She put some money into my shirt pocket. I tried to tell her I didn't need it, but she wouldn't listen. Blake came over and patted me on the back.

"Love you, bud," he said.

"I love y'all too," I said and smiled. With that, I got into my truck and drove over to pick her up.

When I pulled up to her house, she was already waiting on her front porch for me to pick her up. I got out of the truck, and she came over and hugged me. My night was already getting to a great start. She was wearing blue jeans and a hoodie and absolutely looked beautiful. I opened the passenger door for her, and we went off. She lived in Millville not too far from where I was staying. Lobster House was almost an hour's drive. The reason I picked this place was for the long drive, so I'd have a longer time for us to be able to talk.

"I love seafood!" she explained when I told her where we were heading. This made me even happier. "Do you mind if I put some music on for the drive down there?"

"I don't mind at all," I said and flashed her a smile. She turned on my radio, and Hank Williams started playing. I loved Hank when I was younger. He definitely wasn't the most romantic for a first date, though.

"You can change it if you want," I said.

"No, it's fine. My dad listens to this music a lot. I don't mind it," she said.

We mostly made small talk throughout the drive there. I mostly listened to her talk about her day, and she talked about school and work. For the most part, I just sat and listened. I talked about school, too, and my friends. Things seemed to be going well until halfway there. It had been a while since I ate. My stomach started to growl, and I felt pains in my adnominal area. I placed my right hand on my stomach in pain while my left hand gripped the steering wheel. It felt like my stomach was being tightened up.

"Are you okay?" she asked.

"Yeah, I'm fine," I lied. "I was doing sit-ups earlier, so I'm a little sore."

"For our date?" she said, laughing. I couldn't help but smile at her. Things seemed to be going great so far.

By the time we got to the restaurant, I felt so hungry I couldn't help myself. She ordered seafood pasta. I tried to drink a couple of sodas before the waiter took our order. I was hoping it would make me feel fuller, so I wouldn't eat a lot of food, but it didn't help. I didn't want to order a lot of food, but I couldn't help myself. I ordered an appetizer and a large meal. I couldn't help but think to myself that this wasn't me. I didn't understand what was happening to me and why I couldn't just calmly eat a meal. Even during a date.

"Tell me more about yourself," I asked. "I'd love to get to know you more."

"What do you want to know?" she asked.

"Anything," I said. "What do you do for fun? How do you know Lilly?" I was trying to focus on her and not eating. Not my weight right now. I wanted to have a good night, and I didn't want this to ruin it.

"Well, for starters, I love drawing and writing. I do a lot of artwork for church, and a couple of my drawings are actually hanging up in the youth room at church. My youth pastor bought them off me. That's also where I met Lilly. So mostly right now my life has been packed with choosing what colleges I want to go to, finishing up senior year, and doing things with church. How about you?"

"Well, as you could see from the party, I mainly hang out with Brandon. I'm in the choir at high school, and I work part-time. But besides that, not much. I go running too. I promise you, I only drank at the party. That's not something I do normally."

"So you don't throw beer on random girls all the time?" she asked, laughing.

"Nope!" I exclaimed. "I gotta admit, you're the first girl I threw my beer on."

She started laughing. "Do you go to church at all?" she asked.

"I haven't been in a while. I used to go with my mom before she…well, you heard."

She nodded and reached her hand across the table and grabbed mine. My heart started racing. We sat there for a couple of seconds in the quiet. Tears almost started flowing from my eyes. *Don't let her see you cry,* I thought, and I changed the subject.

"What church do you go to?" I asked.

"United Methodist," she said. "Do you believe in God?" She sipped her water.

That was the first time someone actually has asked me that before. I was always raised Christian by my mom, but my dad never practiced. He believed but was one of the worst people I knew. If he was a Christian, I knew I didn't want to be anything like him. My mind raced. I wanted to believe, but with everything that was going on, I couldn't see how a loving God could let any of the things that happened to me happen, let alone happen at the same time. There couldn't be. If there was, I doubted if He cared about someone like me. My mom did nothing but go to church and pray, and look what happened to her.

"No," I said in a voice as soft as silk. I shook my head in silence. "I don't. Well, I try. I try to believe. I just have a hard time doing so, if that makes sense?"

"Absolutely," she said.

I went to say something else, but before I could, the food was brought over to the table. I ordered a crab plate and vegetables, and she ordered seafood pasta. The second my meal and appetizer got placed in front of me, I could already get the feeling of being nervous. I grabbed my stomach, and I couldn't help but feel disgusted with myself. What would Anna think if she saw me eat this much?

"I know you said you don't really believe, but if you don't mind, I'm going to say grace," she said.

"Go ahead," I said. While she bowed her head and started praying, I tried my best to focus on her and to not think about the food. I took one deep breath, and when she finished, I started eating with her. *You're okay,* I thought. *It'll be fine.* I took small bites of my appetizer, and I started to calm down. It had been a while since I actually ate a normal meal. Maybe it wouldn't hurt me. *I'll be okay,* I thought.

"My dad works for a land surveying company, and my mom is a teacher in Vineland High School," she said. "I'm not fully sure what exactly I want to do with animals when I graduate, but I know I want to work with them."

"Is that something you're good at?" I asked. "Working with animals, I mean."

"Well, I get along with my dog well, so I'd like to think it's something I'm good at," she said, chuckling. "But besides that, I'm really good at playing guitar and drawing, as I mentioned earlier. How about you? What are your hobbies?"

While thinking about the food, I started to feel unconfident about myself. I felt bad about how I looked. I needed to say something that would make me sound confident in myself.

"I recently started to get into exercising," I said. "Nothing much, but I started to go running around my neighborhood."

"That's good! I know I need to start doing something like that, but I don't have much motivation to do so." She started laughing. I made myself sound good, and I heard her laugh. *That's what I'm looking for.*

First dates, from my experience, are either a hit or a miss. But there's nothing more enjoyable than them. Getting to know someone, learning about their likes and dislikes. I'd been on bad dates, and I'd been on good ones. Even when a date didn't go as planned and I knew from the start that there wouldn't have been a second one, getting to know someone else was always a fun experience for me. Talking to Anna right there, though, I knew there was going to be a second date, at least on my part. The way the light from the restaurant lit her eyes up, the way it shone off her dark hair. We sat and talked and ate for about forty minutes. Time flies by so quickly on a first date, especially when things are going the way you want them to.

"You look beautiful tonight," I said while smiling at her. She smiled back and blushed while looking down at her plate. Which honestly made her look even cuter.

"Thank you. You don't look too bad yourself," she said.

I looked down at my plate and noticed that most of my food was gone. When that happened, it hit me all over again. I went from focusing on her to focusing on my plate again. *What did I do?* I thought. *I just ate all that food.* I started to get nervous. *No, not here. Things are going really well. I can't let this happen. Not on a date.* I picked up what was left of my soda, and I started to drink it really fast, hoping it would help to calm me down. But it wasn't working. Right as I thought about panicking, I remembered what I did before. I could vomit, but in a restaurant bathroom? I knew I shouldn't be doing this at all, let alone in a public setting. I couldn't sit here and continue to stress in front of Anna, though. I could only hide this from her for so long.

"Excuse me," I said.

I got up and started walking to the bathroom. I went in and looked in the mirror above the sink. All I could think of myself was that I looked disgusting. No one would love me; no one could love me looking the way that I did. *You have to do this.* I turned around and went into the stall. No one was in the bathroom, so I had to do this quickly before someone would come in. Very quickly, I tried to purge, but little came up. I tried harder, but the harder I tried, the more pressure was put on my face. I could feel my face turn red, and tears poured out of my eyes as I did. The soda came up with food at first, but I knew not everything did. I tried one more time and failed and dropped to my knees, coughing. My throat was burning, and I couldn't help but cough like someone was just strangling me. I felt shame. *My throat is on fire,* I thought to myself. I stood up and started to think about Anna and her smile. Everything after that made me happy. The thought of her cheered me up.

I flushed the toilet and went out and washed my hands and threw cold water on my face to make the redness in my face and eyes go away, and I went back to the table. I knew I had to get healthy; I hadn't been doing this long, but I could already feel the negative consequences of this. I remembered reading about eating disorders in health class a couple of years ago. This couldn't be it, though. Not me. This couldn't happen to me. *This is the last time,* I thought to myself. *You have this under control. Starting tomorrow, you will eat right. No more vomiting.* I promised myself this.

She was still sitting there, and when she saw me, her face lit up again.

"Here's the bill," the waiter said. I took it from him and sat back down.

"Thank you so much," she said, smiling.

"You're welcome," I said.

"Hey, Larry," she said. "I know we are in Cape May, so instead of going straight home after this, how would you feel about going for a walk on the beach?" I used to go running on the beach all the time before my mom died. A walk on the beach sounded good. A walk on the beach with her sounded even better.

"I know the perfect spot," I said, smiling. I put the gift card and a good tip on top of the bill, and she stood up and reached her hand down.

"Lead the way," she said. I grabbed her hand, and we walked outside hand in hand. The night wasn't even over, but I knew I didn't want it to end.

There was a section of the beach and Cape May most people didn't know about. There was a strip of beach that you could only get to by a trail. When you got on the beach, it went down about half a mile, and then you came to a jetty made from stones. Farther out into the ocean was the Coast Guard base. If you walked far enough on the jetty, you could see their ships and equipment. If you took your boat out from the loading dock, you'd even go by the Coast Guard base. Most people who came on this part of the beach were bird-watchers and fishermen who walked out onto the jetty. Right after the fishing season ended, though, in October and birds started to leave, you'd never see anyone out here. Usually, just a local who was out for a run with their dog here and there. For the most part, this place was empty. Luckily for me, though, when we got there, no one else was there. It wasn't cold, but it was chilly. The sun was starting to set, and Anna and I walked down the beach, hand in hand.

"This is my favorite spot in the world," I said.

"You haven't been out of Jersey much, have you?" She chuckled and smiled. She turned and sat down on the beach; we were about halfway to the jetty. I sat down next to her. I was glad we stopped. From where I wasn't eating as much as I should, the walk was starting to make me short of breath. The answer to that question was no, I hadn't been out of New Jersey yet in my life. My family vacations were always in Cape May, and besides that, I didn't have any family outside of the state. Every time I wanted to "get away," I always came here.

"I used to come here a lot to go running before Mom died," I said. "Whenever I was stressed about something or wanted to celebrate something, this was the place I'd go to. Of course, after a while, I got used to this being my regular spot. I don't normally bring any friends here. I usually come here to get away from everything, to go fishing, to relax. Things like that."

"Do you ever plan on leaving New Jersey?" she asked.

"I'm not sure. I don't have much here anymore besides my sister, but I don't hate it here. I might look at some colleges outside of the state, or even possibly military, but there's nowhere specific that I want to go."

"I want to leave one day," she said. "In my career, I want to move. Maybe even study abroad. I want to see different parts of the country and what they have to offer. There's so much in the world to see. Like the northern lights, or somewhere tropical. They're not places that I want to live or anything, but they're places that I want to visit."

"The world doesn't look so bad from where I'm sitting," I said while looking at her. She rested her head on my shoulder, and I put my arm around hers. The sun was right about to set. We were quiet for a moment. We sat, watched the sun start to go down. I could see boats and ships on the far horizon. Everything from the beautiful, clear sky to the sun setting, to the sandy beach and the birds flying. It was as beautiful as a Bob Ross painting. Everything I'd been through and every problem I had slowly faded away. I took my phone out with my arm still wrapped around her and put on the first love song I could find on my phone.

"I love this song," she said. She moved even closer to me, and I wrapped both arms around her. We leaned back. I lay down in the sand, and she lay next to me and put her head on my chest. She hummed along with the song right until the end. When the song ended, she looked up at me. I stared into her eyes, and we kissed. There's something about young love. Sure, it's blind. Most people who are mature probably won't catch feelings as strong as we did for each other on our first date. But nothing could have ruined our night together. Not even my new problem.

When the sun was fully set, we headed back to my truck hand in hand. I drove her back home, and we held hands while I drove, the heat slightly on while the radio played whatever country song came on. I dreaded the moment I would have to say good night but looked forward to the kiss good night.

# CHAPTER 7

Monday morning, I woke up ready to face anything thrown at me. I was ready to go back to school, and I had a new and better attitude to do so. Right before I got ready to go back to school, I went and stepped on the scale, and it read 182 pounds. I stepped off the scale and looked into the mirror. I was just wearing my boxers, and I got to say, I didn't get it. I worked so hard to get down; 180 was my original goal weight, but I still felt heavy. I still didn't look the way I wanted to look. *Maybe I need to lose more,* I thought to myself. But I didn't want to continue making myself sick. But I don't know what to do. The more I thought about it, the more I got upset. I started to feel horrible again, and my good attitude started to fade. I sat down next to the scale and hugged my knees, and tears started to roll down my eyes. *If I wasn't good enough for my dad, how will I be good enough for anyone else?* More tears rolled down my face in confusion of what I was going to do about my weight.

There was a knock on the door.

"Yeah?" I said. I tried my best to cover up the tears and cracks in my voice. It was Blake.

"Hey, bud. Are you okay in there?" he asked.

"Ugh." I stood up and started putting my clothes on as fast as I could. "Yeah, I'm fine. Why?"

"I could hear you sniffing in there. It sounded like you were upset is all," Blake replied.

"No, I'm fine," I told him. I started to wipe tears from my eyes, and I went over and opened the door to see him standing there with Emily. I walked out of the bathroom to greet them.

"Good morning," I said.

"You don't look so good," Blake said. "Are you feeling okay?"

"What do you mean?" I asked.

"Well," Emily said, "we've noticed a few things different about you is all. You're spending a lot of time in your room, you've been pulling your pants up a lot from them starting to sag on you…"

"Right now, you look extremely pale," Blake said. "Now, we don't want it to seem like we are attacking you or targeting you in any way. We just want to make sure you're all right."

"Yeah, I'm fine," I said. "There isn't anything to worry about."

I knew I was lying. Over the weekend, I only ate twice. One of those meals didn't stay down either. Things with Anna went well, sure, but I still felt horrible. I was even two pounds over my target weight, and I didn't see any real physical difference in how I looked. I felt horrible mentally and physically, but I couldn't admit that to them. I didn't want them to worry. I had this eating problem, whatever this eating problem was, under control. I didn't need them to worry when I could stop myself anytime I wanted.

"I appreciate you guys checking in on me, but I promise I'm okay." We looked at one another for a moment of silence.

"When was the last time you ate something?" Blake asked.

"Well, yesterday," I said. "I plan on eating breakfast at school, too, when I get there. The reason I've been losing weight is that I've been running a lot more than normal."

"I think you should see a counselor," Blake said. "I know it's probably not something that you want to do, b—"

"I don't want to go to one," I said quickly. "Guys, I promise, I'm fine."

"Larry." Emily started talking and began to choke up. "You've been through a lot. And for someone your age who's already going through a lot with graduating soon and trying to figure out what you want to do with your life, it's all building up on you. We've lost so much. We don't want to lose you too." At this point, she started to wipe tears from her eyes. It took every bit of me from crying too. I held in tears the best I could, and I succeeded at it too. I continued to bottle it up. It was hard enough to see her cry; I couldn't let them see me cry in front of them, too, on top of that.

"I understand your concern, guys," I told them. "Really, I do. But I need y'all to trust me. I'm taking care of myself. If it makes you feel better to see me eat, why don't we order food tonight? We could order a pizza or get takeout. I'll pay."

"That sounds good. We can rent a movie or something too," Blake said.

"Okay. I'm sorry," Emily said. "Look, we will give you trust until you give us a reason not to. If we find out, though, that things aren't okay, will you promise us that you will go see a counselor, even if it's just your school counselor?"

"Yeah," I said. "I promise."

Emily came over and hugged me and told me she loved me. I told her I loved her back. Blake came over and patted me on the back.

"We love you, buddy," he said, and he walked away. I went back to my bedroom and started to get ready for school.

I had to do something. I wanted to continue to lose weight, but I couldn't hurt myself. Especially if Blake and Emily were starting to catch on that something wasn't right. I couldn't continue to hurt myself with whatever this was. *I don't have an eating disorder,* I kept telling myself. *I don't have an addiction.* I looked at my phone and saw there was a good-morning text from Anna:

*Good morning (:*

I texted her back and started driving to school.
I understood Blake and Emily cared about me, but a million thoughts started running through my head. I could stop what I was doing at any given time; I knew I could. But I didn't want to. I wanted to get thinner. I had to get thinner. I had to get into better shape than what I was in right now. I looked awful, and I knew it. This was the only thing I had control over, and I didn't want to lose it.
Weeks went by, and things didn't get better when it came to what I was doing to myself. I researched what I was doing and found out I was struggling with bulimia. The more weight I tried to lose, the more I felt disgusted with the way I looked. I got into the habit of trying my best at trying not to eat. I would go a full day, sometimes two days, without eating. But I would lose self-control; the urge to want to eat would build up inside me to the point I couldn't help myself from eating anymore and instead of eating a normal-size meal, I'd binge an entire meal—I'd eat until I couldn't physically take in any more food. Right after I stopped eating all the food that I binged, I felt guilty. I felt strong guilt because I failed in my attempt to not eat anything. The experience and the guilt I felt was like the feeling you get when you tell your significant other or a friend something you deeply

regret, but worse, this was one of the worst feelings that I ever had emotionally.

The feeling of guilt was enough to make me shake, sweat, and even cry at times. I could feel my stomach bloat, and I felt disgusted with myself when I was done. More disgusted with myself than before I started eating. I'd look into the mirror, and all I could see was a fat slob who failed again to attempt to not eat. I failed all over again. The urge to want to get rid of what I ate would build up stronger than the urge to want to eat to begin with. This led to me vomiting up what I ate, or "purging," as websites would call it. I would force myself to throw up everything I ate. I used my fingers and put them down my throat, and the more I did, the more I could feel my heart slowly start to fall apart. My face turned beet red, and tears and snot started to roll down my face. What I did do was keep track of the very first thing I ate, something that was a different color than the rest of the food I ate, or even something brighter than the rest of the food. So when I saw that come back up, I knew I was finished and almost everything I ate did come back up.

Afterward, my throat burned, and I couldn't stop coughing. Some nights, especially if my binge and purge were late at night, I sat next to the toilet, hugging my knees and crying. I'd cry and cough, and I didn't know how to handle myself. I knew what I was doing was wrong. I was hurting myself and needed help, but I couldn't pull myself to tell anyone. Brandon wouldn't understand, and I couldn't tell Emily anything to make her cry. It would be selfish for me to tell her anything that would upset her any further, wouldn't it? I could have also talked to Blake about it, but he would just tell me to go see a counselor. I couldn't do that; talking to a counselor was the very last thing that I wanted to do.

My weight continued to drop the way I wanted it to. It started to slow down, but it was still dropping at a normal speed. If my weight wasn't dropping at all, I did other things like went running more or even took laxatives a couple of times to get it to start dropping faster. Over the weeks, though, the one thing I had that constant, though, was Anna. We drew closer to each other over the weeks. I brought her over to meet my sister and Blake, and they loved her. I didn't get a chance to meet her parents yet, though. We didn't tell each other yet, but I knew I loved that girl. Though it was because I loved her that I didn't tell her about my problem either. I didn't know how she'd react to it. I didn't know if she'd freak out or not. One thing was for sure, though: out of everything that was going on and had happened, I didn't want to lose her.

I still hadn't told her about my dad either. I knew I would have to sooner or later, but I kept that on the back burner for now. Though one thing scared me most of all: Brandon knew something was up, because he saw vomit from where I left some behind at the party. Blake and Emily knew something was up, too, from the way I'd been acting. I was doing my best to hide this from everyone, but more than my health, I was more concerned about them finding out about this. I could only hide it for so long before they caught me purging. I just wanted to ride it out as long as I could.

# CHAPTER 8

"Are you sure you're going to be okay here by yourself?" Emily asked.

"Yeah, I'll be fine," I said.

Today was Thanksgiving. Emily and Blake were going over to my dad's house for Thanksgiving dinner, and I would have rather spent it alone than go have Thanksgiving with my dad.

"You're sure you don't want to come?" Emily asked.

"Yeah, I'm positive!" I exclaimed sarcastically. "Like I want to spend the holiday with the same man who not only threw me out but also hasn't even so much as called me since."

"All right, hun, you ready to go?" Blake said, walking out of the kitchen with a pie. "I'll be waiting in the car."

Emily walked over to me.

"I'm fine," I said in a softer voice. "I'll just relax here and trash-talk Brandon when the Cowboys lose the game."

She hugged me and told me she'd bring a plate back if there were any leftovers. The moment she left, I walked over and fell on the couch and turned the television on and scrolled troughed Netflix. Thanksgiving at my house was always my parents, sister, and close family. Like my mom's sister and my dad's brothers. My dad and uncles would drink beer and surround the television, watching a football game while their wives and my mom would cook and set dinner up. But not only did I not want to see my dad, I also just couldn't do Thanksgiving without my mom there. I was already in a sad mood spending the first major holiday without my mom; I didn't need to confront my dad on top of that. I put on *How I Met Your Mother* reruns on Netflix and started to fall asleep when Anna called me.

"Hey, babe," I said, answering the phone.

"Hey, hun! Happy Thanksgiving," she said.

"You too," I replied. "What are you doing to celebrate?"

"It's just me and my parents today. I believe they're having some friends over, but not much. How about you?"

"Watching the Cowboys game and possibly eating a plate when my sister gets back home," I told her.

"Back home?" she asked. "Where are they?"

I lied and told her that they went to spend Thanksgiving with their coworkers. That they were having a "Friendsgiving" and I didn't want to intrude on them even though they insisted that I come and join them.

"Are you spending Thanksgiving alone?" she asked.

"Yeah," I told her.

"No, you're not," she told me. "Come over to my house. You'll have dinner with me and my parents."

Before I could say anything to her, she said she was going to hang up before I could say no and that I should be over at her house in an hour. With that, she hung up. I was still wearing sweats and a T-shirt, so I jumped out of bed as fast as I could and ran to go get a shower and change into decent clothes. Before I jumped into the shower, I ran over and stepped on the scale: 168 pounds. I couldn't believe it; I'd lost a lot of weight so far, and I couldn't believe that I made this much progress. I got a big smile on my face then went to look in the mirror. Despite how happy I was from the weight drop, I still knew that I looked fat.

*You cannot purge tonight,* I told myself in the mirror. *Eat light. Don't purge at Anna's house.* I didn't want to. It was my first time meeting her parents, and I didn't want them in the slightest bit to know that I had a problem. I needed their approval. I put on my nicest pair of blue jeans, a button-up shirt, and my boots and headed over to her house. The second I got to her house, she was already outside. When I pulled up, she ran over to my truck and hugged me. I kissed her.

"I'm so excited for you to meet my parents," she kept saying as she rushed me into her house. "By the way, my dad is a Cowboys fan. Act like one to get along with him better," Anna added.

Her dad was a tall man. He was more built in the arms and shoulders, but he had a small gut. He had a button-up shirt on that he kept tucked in. He had a five o'clock shadow and a cross necklace wrapped around his neck. *A Christian.*

"Hello," he said, reaching his hand out. "I'm Doug. You must be Larry."

"Yes, sir," I said, shaking his hand. "It's nice to meet you."

"It's nice to meet you as well," he said with a straight face. "You're a thin fellow. I remember being that skinny. Enjoy it while you can, because when you get to be my age, well…" He grabbed his stomach and started laughing.

"Come have a seat, Larry!" he said. "The Cowboys game is getting ready to start!"

"I love the Cowboys!" I exclaimed and looked at Anna. She covered her mouth to prevent herself from laughing. Brandon at this point was blowing my phone up with texts about the game too. *It's going to be a long night,* I thought to myself.

We went through the whole nine yards of meeting your girlfriend's dad. He asked me about my goals in life, what intentions I had with dating his daughter, and what he expected from me. While Anna and her mom were preparing dinner, he also went over things about Anna that she hadn't told me yet. Things like flowers she liked and so on.

"I'm just trying to earn you some cool points with her," he said, laughing. I seemed to be getting along with him really well, especially compared to my last girlfriend's dad. He was one of the types of dads where he didn't say much, never laughed at your jokes, and you didn't know if he hated you or not. You just sat wondering if he did and you would even be okay if he told you flat out he hated you, because at that point, at least he was saying something.

Anna's dad seemed to love me; there was something about him that made him seem happy. I don't know whether he was putting on a show, or maybe it was just his faith. But there was definitely something about him that made him positive.

This year, the Cowboys were playing against the Chargers; my guess was the Cowboys were going to lose, but Branon and Doug both seemed to feel positive about their outcome. Spoiler alert: they lost, big-time. We obviously didn't know that yet, though.

"Dinner is ready!" Anna yelled from the kitchen.

"Awesome!" Doug said, standing up. "C'mon, Larry, all of us are going to make plates, and we can eat out in the living room while the game is on." We walked over to the kitchen.

"Hey, darling," Anna's mom said. "I'm Rebekah." She took my hand and shook it gently. She showed me around the kitchen and showed me all the food they had prepared. There was a lot of it. Standing in the kitchen, just looking at the food, I started to feel nervous. My hands started shaking a little bit.

"If you excuse me, I'm going to go wash my hands in the bathroom, if that's fine?" I asked.

"No problem at all," Doug said. "Go through the living room and go down the hall. You'll see it."

I started down for the bathroom and bent over the sink. I started throwing water in my face. I knew I couldn't "just eat light" as I thought I did before. I knew I was going to end up eating a lot. I washed my hands and tried to calm myself. I was so used to just binging and purging or having a small snack to keep my energy up, not eating a normal-size meal. It would ruin everything. I started breathing out of my mouth until I was fully calm. I dried my face and walked back out into the kitchen.

"Here you go, babe," Anna said, handing me a plate. I made one for you while you were in the bathroom. I was relieved. I knew if I made my own plate, I would overdo it drastically, or underdo it.

"Hun, why don't you make me a plate?" Doug asked.

"You're too picky," she said, laughing. "Boy git."

The family friends that Anna made mentioned of never showed up, so it was just us. As the game progressed, it was more and more clear that the Cowboys weren't going to win.

"You said you 'loved the Cowboys.' I hope you didn't put money on this game," Doug said. I turned my head and looked at Anna and smiled.

"Oh no, I didn't," I said, and Anna covered her mouth again, trying not to laugh. I also made notice that the text messages from Brandon about "his boyz" winning became less and less.

"Well, they're not going to win," Doug said. "I'm getting another plate. You in, Larry?"

"Sure…," I said, not wanting to disappoint my girlfriend's dad.

"Attaboy," Doug said. "You can use more meat on those bones."

As we started walking toward the kitchen, the hope started to fall from my face that tonight would be easy and that I wouldn't overdo it. Doug got another big plate, and as I started making my plate, I tried to only get a little.

"C'mon, you can eat more than that. If we leave too many leftovers, I'll eat it all, and that won't be good," he said. *It won't be good for me either,* I thought to myself. I threw more food on the plate and grabbed another can of Coke. I walked back to the living room. At this point, I could already hear Brandon saying, "We still dem, boy" or "He's still a Cowboys fan until he dies." Because there was no way they'd be able to catch up this far into the game.

"Make sure y'all are saving room for dessert," Rebekah said. She and Anna were walking into the kitchen to get another plate of food as well.

I didn't want to purge. I really didn't want to purge. Not here. But between two huge plates, and now hearing about desserts, it all became overwhelming again. I started to throw down the food fast. Afterward, I washed down the Coke. I even went back into the kitchen to grab more turkey and mac and cheese. I must admit, even though I didn't plan on eating much, Rebekah was great at cooking. I threw down my third plate, and afterward, I was full.

"I wish I could eat that much and stay skinny," Doug said. "I guess that kind of stuff disappears with age. The Cowboys aren't gonna win tonight. That's depressing, but the wife made a pecan and pumpkin pie tonight. It tastes good with vanilla ice cream on top and a cup of coffee. You a coffee drinker, Larry?"

"You know it!" I replied. "I'm going to go use the bathroom really quickly before dessert."

He nodded.

I went to the bathroom and threw up. I wanted to make sure that there was no sign from me doing that in here, though. When I finished, I flushed the toilet. I put cold water on my face and took deep breaths until every bit of redness in my face and in my eyes was gone, and then I blew my nose. After that, I sprayed air freshener and washed my hands again to make sure there wasn't any smell of vomit. I flushed the toilet a couple more times and even scrubbed around the toilet bowl to make sure that there wasn't any vomit around that. Everything looked better.

I looked in the mirror again to be double sure that there wasn't any redness in my eyes. I also borrowed some mouthwash from them and rinsed my mouth out so they couldn't smell any vomit coming off my breath. *Perfect,* I said to myself. I put the toilet bowl down and sat down on it. I put my face into my hands and tried to think over everything I just did. My entire life right now was unhealthy, and what I was doing to cover everything up made it even more unhealthy. It was only a matter of time before someone caught me, and then I was in big trouble when I had to explain. I put my head up and sighed. I shook my head and thought to myself that it was what it was, and I went back out to meet them in the kitchen. Pie and coffee—I could handle that.

"Well, Larry!" Doug said when I walked back into the kitchen. "I and the missus are gonna go lie in bed and watch television. We'll let you kids enjoy the living room and give y'all some alone time." He stuck out his hand, and I shook it.

"It was nice meeting you," I told him.

"It sure was!" He leaned in and said in a lower voice, "Remember, I'll trust you until you give me a reason not to."

"Yessir." I shook my head.

"What happened to your hand?" he asked.

"What?" I said in confusion. I looked at my hand, and my knuckles were beet red. It appeared to have marks in it as well. "Ouch."

"Did you hit your hand on something?" he asked. I started to struggle to think of a story, so I said the first thing that came to mind.

"Yeah, I hit it on the bathroom sink by accident. I scraped it on the sink when I went to go wash my hands," I said. If he didn't buy that, honestly, I couldn't blame him. I had to come up with something, though.

"That's funny. Try to be more careful." He chucked and picked up his plate with a slice of pie and vanilla ice cream and a cup of coffee, and Rebekah came to give me a handshake as well, and they left for their bedroom. Anna came toward me with two plates of pie and kissed me.

"I'm glad you finally got to meet them," she said. "Let's go eat and go for a walk." That sounded nice. We did just that.

It was dark and chilly out. I grabbed a hoodie out of my truck, and Anna ended up putting it on. I had another flannel, so it was okay. We started to walk up the quiet streets of suburban Millville. The streetlights lit up the road, and on occasion, a car drove past, but overall, the night was quiet, and it was ours.

"Can I ask you something?" Anna said. She took ahold of my hand and looked up at me. "If you don't feel comfortable answering this, it's fine. I just need to know."

"What is it?" I asked.

"You said your mom died. I'm really sorry to hear that. But you introduced me to your sister and her husband, but not your dad. I know it's probably none of my business, but I was wondering where your dad is at. Is he still alive?"

I thought for a few seconds. If I should tell her the truth. Should I tell her a lie, which was probably better for her to hear? If I was being honest with myself, a lie was what I wanted to hear. I hadn't seen or even heard from my dad since he threw me out.

"I don't know where my dad is," I said. I technically wasn't lying. I didn't know where he was in that moment of time. He could be drunk on the couch or sitting at the table with Emily at Blake. Who knew? I continued telling my half-truths. "He and my mom aren't together. I lost touch with him a while back. I don't talk to him anymore. So after my mom passed, I moved in with my sister."

"Oh, I'm sorry to hear that," she said. "I know you've been through a lot lately. I just want to make sure you're all right."

"I'm all right when I'm around you," I told her. I squeezed her hand a little tighter. She stood still for a moment. I started walking a little farther, but when I saw she stopped, I did, too, and turned around and looked at her.

"Hey, I love you," she said.

My heart felt like it skipped. You know, time is a weird thing. When you're having fun, time can fly by like seconds. When you're bored, it drags by the current in the ocean. But when you feel that moment when you get bad news or extremely good news, time, just for a second, you lose track of. Between the way the streetlight lit up her red hair and her beautiful "kiss me" smile, the time that time disappeared when I heard her say those words. I went over to her and wrapped my arms around her.

"I love you too," I whispered.

She buried her head into my chest, and I rested my chin on the top of her head. It's a wonderful feeling when you're that much taller than your significant other. Right under that stoplight, she looked up at me and I bent over slightly to kiss her. My world was spinning, and I remember thinking that if there was a god, he was throwing me a prize in that current moment.

# CHAPTER 9

I was sitting in the gym locker room. I weighed in at 163 pounds. After the weekend, I didn't eat much. Just a few snacks. I ate a few full-size meals and vomited one of them. I was feeling a little tired, but nothing out of the normal. Feeling tired, unfortunately, was becoming the new normal for me. To start boosting my energy, I turned to drink more energy drinks. I was drinking one every morning when I woke up, and the midafternoon, either before going to work or going for my run, I downed a second one. I was getting so dependent on caffeine to keep me going that if I stopped drinking them, I would get headaches. On top of that, I was feeling disappointed with myself. My current weight wasn't horrible, in my opinion. My weight was still dropping, but every time I looked in the mirror, all I could see was someone I didn't want to see. I felt that I looked disgusting and fat. The more I looked in the mirror, the worst I felt about myself. Gym didn't start for a few minutes, so I sat in the locker room by myself while my classmates filed in. I sat down on the bench in front of my locker, looking down at my lap.

"What's going on, ghost?" I looked up and saw Tanner. I got a smile on my face.

"What did you call me?" I said, chuckling.

"Ghost," he said. "I haven't heard from you much lately, and you're starting to get pale. So the ghost it is." He started laughing and reached out his hand. I took it, and he pulled me up to my feet.

"You tall bastard," he said, laughing. "We're gonna mess with Brandon, right?"

"You know it!" I said, laughing. As bad as I was just feeling, I could always count on Tanner or Brandon to bring a smile to myself. It's hard to be down when your friends are constantly trying to lift you up.

Brandon walked into the locker room. Of course, he was wearing his Dallas Cowboys hoodie. He made it too easy sometimes.

"We dem boyz!" Tanner screamed at him as he came in, waving his arms back and forth.

"We *are* dem boyz!" I screamed at him, too, while holding Tanner's shoulders and jumping up and down. Brandon threw his hat at us.

"You can both bite me!" he yelled back at us, laughing. "Both of you must think you're real funny!"

We both started laughing while I changed into my gym sweatpants and sneakers. Since gym was the last class of the day, I never bothered to change my shirt for gym. I was going home or to work afterward, anyway, so there wasn't any point. I didn't have to change for a different class.

"Besides the Cowboys not winning, my Thanksgiving was actually pretty good," Brandon said. "I ate a lot of food and took a good nap. I got a little holiday bonus from work too." Lucky for him, the only thing I got was cut hours because my job was closed because of the holiday."

"I went to Anna's house and met her parents," I said.

"How'd that go?" he asked.

"Well, her dad thinks I'm a Cowboys fa—"

"Yeah, buddy!" he yelled. "I'm sorry, continue."

"It seemed really nice," I said. "It gave me a feeling of belonging to a family again, and I don't know, I…I guess I felt normal again. Like I'm fine now. But I forgot what it was like to be around an actual family again. Not just my sister and Blake."

"I guess that makes sense. We're not enough for you anymore," Tanner said jokingly. "You need a girl to make you feel loved. I'm just playing. I know what you mean."

I laughed a little.

We joked around more in the locker room while waiting for class to start. When the bell rang, Tanner started walking out, and I sat down and sighed.

"You okay?" Brandon asked.

"Yeah, I'm fine, I suppose." I explained to him a little bit that I was trying to change my body to get into better shape. I didn't mention that I was vomiting or skipping meals; I just added that I was working out a lot and I wasn't seeing the results that I wanted. I wanted to gain muscle, but I was only losing weight. Which wasn't fully false. I wanted to be stronger; I just didn't want to eat. I was talking to Brandon using the half-truth method that I used to talk to Anna.

"I can understand that," Brandon said. "You know, at Planet Fitness, I use a workout routine that I found to be effective. If you want, you can start coming with me and we can start working out together. I can show you what to do."

"That would be great!" I exclaimed.

I hopped up to my feet, and I started to feel light-headed when I did. I leaned against the locker a little bit so Brandon couldn't tell something was wrong. My vision started to get blurry on top of that; it only lasted a few seconds before going away. Maybe I was just dehydrated. I'd make sure to get plenty of water before starting class. I shook it off like it was nothing. We started to head to class. The thought excited me that I would get to go to the gym and work out with my best friend. I'd gain muscle and lose weight at the same time, I thought to myself. Little did I know back then, though, that was not how fitness and the human body worked.

# CHAPTER 10

There are two types of people. There are people who wait until after Thanksgiving to start listening to Christmas music and putting Christmas lights up, then some people put Christmas lights up right on November 1, after Halloween. Typically, when December first hits, they get even more pumped up with the Christmas spirit and they're practically Santa Claus undercover. Brandon was this type of person, times twenty. He picked me up from my house going to the gym. We had made a plan on double-dating with Lilly and Anna to the movies when we were done working out. The second Brandon pulled up, I could hear "All I Want for Christmas." He pulled up to my house, and as I approached the car, he turned the music down.

"Really, bro?" I asked, getting into the car.

"Really what?" he asked me.

"I don't know what's weirder, the fact that you're listening to this type of Christmas music or the fact that you're listening to it alone already, before you even pick me up," I told him, laughing.

"Excuse me!" he yelled, laughing, starting to drive away. "But the very last time I checked, Planet Fitness is a judgment-free zone, and I didn't need to be attacked like this," he said, laughing, and punched my arm.

Tanner, Brandon, and I did manage to keep a Christmas tradition alive for the past couple of years, though. The Friday night before Christmas, the three of us guys got together to watch *Die Hard*, only us guys. Mainly because Lilly didn't believe it was a Christmas movie, and after a brief conversation with Anna about it, she didn't either. But Christmas didn't feel like Christmas until us guys watched *Die Hard*. In other words, we were the typical American males.

I didn't weigh myself that morning. I really had to try my best and push myself not to. I typically weighed myself at least twice a day, but I pushed myself not to because I wanted to see if I could surprise myself with losing weight from the gym. I also wanted to see the results from weight lifting; maybe I could build my arms up more. I brought clean clothes to get changed out of when we were done since we were picking up the girls afterward. I brought stuff to get changed into and a simple shower supplies.

We started out with running on the treadmill. Brandon said he didn't typically go running every day when he went to have a workout, but today running was part of the "routine" that he had. He said he typically ran one mile in the beginning, and if he had enough energy when the workout was done, he'd run another mile at the end. On the treadmill, my mile time was six minutes and thirty-ish seconds. It was even better than Brandon's mile time, which secretly made me happier than he'd understand.

"All right, show-off," he said. "I'll have my moment of glory, though, when we start weight lifting."

We worked out our arms today, the triceps, biceps, and we also did forearm workouts. He said he did that at the end of the week. Saturday, if he came, he did legs. He said he saved leg day for Saturday because if he had to miss any day of the week to go to the gym, it was going to be a Saturday. I didn't blame it; to this day, I can't stand to do any leg workouts besides running. Brandon was the best yet worst workout partner you could have. When lifting weights, after every rep, he would say something "inspirational" to keep you going, but his "inspiration" was funny, which made weight lifting extremely difficult.

"One…" I started counting lifting the weight up. Brandon said, "Keep her going big, man."

"Two…!" I counted. "Keep her *flowing* big, man!" Brandon yelled.

*Three!* I counted in my head this time, hoping he wouldn't say anything. He did. "Big man, I said if you want to get those dates, you better pick up that weight!" I did all my reps and put the weights down, looked at him, and laughed.

"Again, really, bro?" I asked. He took out his earbud.

"What?" he said, laughing. I took his earbud out of his hand and looked to see what he was listening to. It was Christmas music again.

"Don't even say anything," he said. I was listening to metal on the radio, with a mixture of classic rock. I thought rock or metal would be better to listen to as workout music, especially better than country, definitely better than Christmas music. No offense to Brandon.

When we finished working out, Brandon said he was skipping running another mile, and we just went to the locker room to get changed. I went to the water fountain and started chugging water down. I felt so thirsty and dehydrated, more than I ever did just going running. I was still breathing heavily, and I was sore in my arms and chest.

"Wow!" Brandon yelled, slamming his locker shut. "I gotta say, Larry, I'm proud of you. You hit it hard today. As a way of celebrating, let's skip leg day tomorrow." He chuckled.

"You bet!" I said. I sat down on a bench in the corner of the gym. I leaned my head back and looked up at the ceiling, trying to catch my breath.

"The first couple of weeks of going will suck. You'll feel the sorest, and even doing things as simple as stretching out your arms fully will hurt. It gets better, though. You just gotta stick through it with me," he told me. He grabbed his bag out of the locker and took his shirt off. I was still sitting down, getting ready to get changed. I took my shoes off and took my shirt off as well.

"Oh my goodness!" Brandon yelled, standing back. "Larry! What happened to you?"

"What?" I said. I got scared for a second that something might have been on me.

"I can see your entire rib cage. You look sick!" he yelled at me. "When was the last time you ate?"

"I eat all the time. What is wrong with you?" I asked in a defensive voice. He started to make me a little angry by questioning me as stern as he was.

"That is not normal!" he yelled. "I'm not trying to bust on you, but you have to eat more. Heavy lifting isn't going to do you any good if you're not eating right. I mean, dude, you're pale as drywall. As skinny as you are, you look like a skeleton!"

I sat in silence. Hearing him say that really started to upset me and make me even more mad. I didn't want to hear this from my best friend.

"I need you to be honest with me, Larry. At my party a while back, that vomit I found in the bathroom, you forced that up, didn't you?" Brandon asked.

"No, I didn't," I lied with a brief hesitation.

"Don't lie to me, Larry!" Brandon started to get even more stern in the way he was talking to me, which started to make me even angrier.

"I wasn't," I said. At this point, I was getting even more defensive and even angrier.

"I know when you're lying, Larry!" he yelled. "I'm just looking out for you!"

I got mad and jumped to my feet as fast as I could.

"I don't need you to tell—"

I stopped talking. I started to feel light-headed again; this time, it was a lot worse than before. My vision started to become blurry. I could feel myself get hot, and everything began to black out.

"Larry?" Brandon asked. "Are you okay? Hey! Bro!" He started to rush toward me, but it was too late. I fell, and my head hit the bench in the middle of the gym locker room. I could faintly hear Brandon yell.

"Larry! Help! Someone call an ambulance!"

I tried my best to breathe, but I slowly started to doze off until I was fully out.

## CHAPTER 11

I woke up again in the back of an ambulance. Brandon was sitting in the back with me, and there was a cuff around my arm, taking my blood pressure. I opened my eyes and looked around. No one noticed I was awake again. For some reason, I didn't want them to either. I closed my eyes shut again and pretended to be still out. I did so until I was sleeping again. I slept for a couple of minutes until the ambulance arrived at the emergency room. Emily was waiting there for our arrival. They pushed me into a room and left for a few minutes, and I fell asleep again. I woke up again to the pinch of a needle going into my arm. A nurse was putting an IV in me. I sat up immediately.

"Don't worry!" she said. "It's all right. I'm just drawing some blood to run a couple of tests, and we're giving you some water and minerals to get your vitamins up." I sat back in the bed and stayed quiet. I looked around the room, not fully remembering why I was here. The nurse started asking me a couple of questions to make sure I was fully stable. My name, birthday, and the last thing I remembered.

"I fell, right? At the gym. I remember standing up too quickly and I fell over," I said.

"Yeah, that's what happened," Brandon confirmed. I was looking up, and he was sitting on the far end of the room. I looked around and saw that Emily was sitting in a chair next to my bed. I looked around to see if anyone else was there—no one. I examined the rest of the room. It was a decent size, a small television. I was still wearing my sweatpants from the gym. I didn't have a shirt on either.

"He fell and hit his head on the bench at the gym," Brandon said. The nurse turned from him again and focused on me.

"That's the last thing I remember. I don't remember much besides waking up a couple of times on my way over here. I don't remember getting put into the ambulance, though. I just remember bits and pieces of the ride over here."

"Very good," she said. "We're going to run a CAT scan, too, to see if everything is okay. In the meantime, sit tight, and your doctor will be in shortly. In the meantime, can you go ahead and put this on for me?" She handed me a hospital robe. I nodded, and she left the room. I turned and looked at Emily, who was wiping tears from her eyes.

"Hey," I told her. "You don't have to cry. Everything is going to be okay. I'm fine."

"Don't tell me you're fine!" she yelled at me through tears. "When we both know you're not!" I sat in silence as I put my hospital robe.

"I knew there was something wrong with you! I just couldn't fully figure out what. When the doctor comes in here and starts asking questions, I need you to be fully honest with him. About everything! Whatever is going on, whatever is wrong with you, you can't hide it from him!" Brandon stated from across the room.

This was why I couldn't tell anyone about what was going on with me. Even though I was suffering, they were yelling and they were mad. At that moment, I couldn't think about telling the doctor the truth. All I could think about were regrets of taking my shirt off around someone else, or that maybe I stood up too fast when arguing with Brandon at the gym. It made me even angrier and irritated. I was the one that was suffering right then, so why was I the one that was being made to feel guilty?

"Does Anna know where I'm at?" I asked.

"That's not important right now," Emily said. "She'll be okay. Just try to relax while the docto—"

"Hello!" The doctor walked in. "I'm Dr. Robbinson. I'm one of the adolescent doctors here."

Emily stood up and introduced herself. Brandon stood up after confirming everything with me would be okay. He came over to my bed and hugged me.

"It'll be okay, bro. Text me when you get discharged from here," he said softly and headed out.

"Your name is Larry?" Dr. Robbinson asked. I said yes. "Okay, Larry, the first thing I'm going to do with you is run some exercises with you to test your strength, okay?" I nodded in agreement. We went through movements with my legs and arms. He had me raise my legs up and down, then move my arms in circles. He then held his hands out and pointed his fingers up and asked me to pull his hands toward him. Then he held out both hands like he was going to give me a high five and asked me to push his hands forward. He then put out his hands with his palms facing up.

"Okay, Larry, now put your hands over mine and push down," Dr. Robbinson said. I did, and as I was doing so, he stopped and was staring at the top of my hands. There was a moment of silence, and he went from looking at my hands to making eye contact with me.

"Okay," he said. "Very good. That's enough for now. Larry, do you mind opening your mouth and saying 'Ah' for me?" I did so, and he grabbed a little mirror that dentists carry and put it in my mouth and looked inside.

"All right," he said. He looked at my sister. "Can I speak to you in the hallway?"

"Of course," Emily said, and they stood up and went into the hallway. *Why did he have to look in my mouth?* I thought to myself. I started to try to think and figure out if he knew or not. It started to make me nervous. They were gone for a few minutes, then the doctor came back in. He was alone, though.

"Okay, Larry, I asked your sister if she could stay down the hall in the waiting lobby while the two of us talked. I figured that this conversation might be easier to have if it's just us guys in the room. It might even be easier for us to talk than to try to talk this over with a friend."

"Okay?" I asked. He came over and sat on the foot of my bed, and I sat up straight to be able to talk with him better.

"I'm going to ask you a question," he said. "No matter how awkward it is, no matter how uncomfortable it makes you feel, I need you to be fully honest with me. Understand?"

"Mhmm," I said while moving my head up and down. *He knows. Crap, he knows. He has to,* I thought to myself.

"How long have you been struggling with bulimia?" he asked. I tried to say that I wasn't, and he cut me off and continued talking. "Cut it out, Larry. Now, you might have everyone else thinking you're not, but you're not going to lie to me. Between how skinny you are, the marks on your knuckles, and the way your teeth look, there's not a shred of doubt that you are. Now, I didn't ask if you are or not—that's perfectly clear to me. I'm asking how long you have been struggling with it."

I sat in silence for a couple of seconds and looked at my lap. The moment I feared had arrived. People knew; if my sister didn't know already, if the doctor didn't tell her in the hallway, he would when we were done talking.

"Since my mom died," I said. Tears started rolling down my face. "The beginning of the school year."

"A few months," he said. "I have to be honest, for only being a few months, it really has done a toll on your body. Look, this is nothing to be ashamed about. I need you to know that. There are plenty of people who struggle with this, and I know it might be difficult, but there is help available."

I wiped tears from my eyes.

"You just have to stop hiding this from people," he said. "Look, how about this? We'll run a CAT scan on your head like we said we would, to make sure you didn't hurt yourself when you fell. Then, I'll have your discharge papers brought up and we'll get you out of here. But while I'm doing that and Mrs. Emily comes back in here, I want you to talk to her about everything that's going on. I'm recommending you to a therapist I know too. We can start getting this worked on, all right?" I nodded, and he patted me on the shoulders and walked out.

A nurse came in and brought me down to get a CAT scan. Everything with my head was fine.

When Emily came in, she sat next to my bed. I was putting my normal clothes back on and my shirt that Brandon brought with him from the gym. My phone was blown up by both Anna and Lilly making sure I was all right. I looked at the time and realized it was too late in the evening to go to the movies. I texted them I was okay, then I turned back and looked at Emily, who was sitting with her hand over her mouth.

"So you have an eating disorder?" she asked.

"Yes," I said, nodding in agreement.

"For how long?" she asked. "I mean, I knew something was wrong, but I just don't…I…how long has this been going on?"

"Since I moved in with you," I said.

The doctor came in with paperwork.

"You're all good to leave," he said. "I'm giving you a referral and a number to a therapist. I trust him, and he's a good guy. I do expect you to go." I took the paperwork, and the doctor nodded at me and told me to get well soon.

Emily and I started to head home. We didn't say a word the entire ride. I continued to text Anna to assure her that I was fine. The drive felt awkward.

Later, I walked into the house, Emily followed, and she finally broke the silence.

"I talked to Dad. I called him when I was on the way to the hospital," Emily said.

"Okay," I replied, and I turned around to face her. "So what did he say about all this?"

"He said, 'So much for raising the bar,'" Emily told me.

"Of course he did." I turned around and continued walking throughout the house. I threw my paperwork from the hospital on the kitchen table. I was hungry but still didn't want to eat, so I grabbed a Coke from the fridge and sat down at the kitchen table. When I got hungry, I drank a soda; it took away the hunger pangs. If that didn't work, then I normally lay down on my fists. That took the hunger pangs away most of the time.

"You need to go to that therapist," Emily said.

"Please," I said. "I can get better on my own. I don't need to go and ha—"

"I don't care!" Emily said, raising her voice. "Blake and I will even pay if the insurance won't cover the full thing, if we have to. This isn't up for discussion. You're going."

"Just give me time to get better. I don't need to go to see any—"

Emily cut me off again. "We tried that already! Remember? You even promised me and Blake that you would go see a counselor if you weren't all right!"

"I'm going to be okay," I tried to tell her. I didn't know if I was lying to her or myself. I knew at this point I had a problem, but I couldn't pull myself to admit it.

"I don't know what you call this!" Emily yelled. "But the very last thing that I would call it is okay! I'm not going to sit here while my younger brother slowly kills himself over something I knew he could have gotten help for. You're going to at least try to go to the counselor, and I'm going to call him tomorrow. End of discussion!" She started to tear up. The dog came out and started barking from the sound of her yelling. Ever since I was younger and she was younger, I could never handle seeing her cry. Maybe it was from me being a protective brother, but seeing her cry was just something I wasn't good at handling.

"Okay," I said. "Okay, I'll go. If you can make the appointment, I promise I'll be there."

Emily came over and hugged me, and I threw my arms around her and held her tightly.

"I'm sorry I'm putting you through this," I told her.

"Please don't be sorry. We'll figure this out," she said. "We've been through a lot, but we can figure this thing out."

I went back to my room and closed the door behind me. I lay in bed for a few minutes, just staring at the ceiling. I didn't know why I didn't want to get help, but I just didn't want to go to a therapist. Even though I knew I needed to, the thought of it just made me uncomfortable.

My phone started ringing; it was Anna.

"Hey, babe!" I said.

"I talked to Brandon and Lilly. I want to hear it from you, though. Are you…do you have an eating disorder or something wrong?" she asked.

*Thanks a lot, Brandon!* I thought to myself.

Anna knowing about this was exactly the last thing I wanted. It was bad enough that he and Emily knew about it, but know Anna and Lilly did too.

"Yeah," I told her. "I'm having a little bit of trouble with it. It's nothing that I can't handle, though. My sister wants me to see a counselor."

"Why didn't you tell me about something like this?" Anna asked. She sounded mad. "This isn't something that you keep to yourself. You need to talk about this kind of stuff with me, with your friends."

"I'm sorry," I said. There wasn't much I could say. As much as I wanted to disagree, I knew she was right; I should have talked to others about this.

"You're going to the counselor, right?" she asked in a stern voice.

"Yeah," I said.

"Larry?" she asked me. "You better not be lying to me."

"I am! I'm going!" I took a couple of seconds and took a deep breath and calmed down. "I'm sorry, it's just Emily and the doctor both have gotten on me about this so far tonight. I need to relax. But I promise you, I'll go." We got into our first argument on me not being "fully honest" with her, and we both yelled and said some things we both were probably going to regret in the morning. But this was just another reason I didn't want to tell anyone I was having this problem.

"Okay," she said. "I trust you. I'll let you get some rest. I'm going to go get ready for bed too."

"I love you, hun," I said.

"I love you too," she said, and she hung up.

I could tell she was mad at me, but there wasn't anything I could do about it tonight. I lay back in bed tonight and continued to look at the ceiling. I didn't eat tonight, but they gave me stuff at the hospital to get my electrolytes and vitamins up. Good enough for me. I shut the lights off and closed my eyes. It only took a few minutes, but I finally fell asleep.

# CHAPTER 12

It took me two weeks to be able to get an appointment with the therapist. He said that first-time appointments were longer than normal appointments, so the cost was a little higher, and it was harder to find the extra hour in his schedule. His name was Dr. Beech. He was a Christian counselor who also taught at the school of ministry in the town next to mine. He was an older man who was also retired for the most part. He had a doctorate in Christian counseling, but even though he called himself a Christian counselor, he still saw people who weren't Christian. He was probably one of the nicest older gentlemen you could meet.

 I wish I could say the last two weeks were easy, but they weren't, not by a long shot. I tried a little to get this under control before I went to see Dr. Beech, but I couldn't. What didn't help either was every time I went to the bathroom at home, I knew either Emily or Blake was listening outside the bathroom door. I could hear them or even see their shadow underneath the door. If I did do something to make myself sick, I did sometimes when I got home from school or work, when they were still at work, or when they were sleeping. I didn't check my weight, though. I hadn't checked it for a while. I was worried about what the scale would tell me after the hospital gave me all those vitamins and liquids, so I wanted to stay off for a while until I felt that I lost what they could have put on me.

Anna and I had some conversations about me and about us as a couple. She apologized for the fight we had, and I did too. It wasn't fair for her to yell at me and get mad when I was the one struggling, and it wasn't fair that I kept something this serious a secret from her and everyone else. Things between us went back to normal, and that made me happy.

I pulled up to the address Dr. Beech gave Emily over the phone. His office was an addition he had put on his house. I walked up the sidewalk to a door with flowerpots on both sides. There was a sign with his name, and it read, "Ring doorbell upon arrival." I did. I was a few minutes early, so it took him a couple of minutes to answer.

"Hello!" he said with a big smile on his face. He was of average height, so like everyone that was of average height, he had to look up to me. "You must be Larry. Come on in." I followed him in, and he walked me over into his office. He had a couch for me to sit on, and in front of me was a Bible and few dishes full of candy, and across the room was a coffeepot.

"Feel free to help yourself," he said, and he sat down in the chair in front of me, putting his glasses on. Before we started, he had me sign some paperwork, and he told me that everything I said here would be fully confidential. He legally could not tell anyone what I told him, unless I shared with him that I had plans on hurting myself or others, then he would legally have to tell someone. He asked me basic questions to start. My full name, age, date of birth, what school I went to, any hobbies I might have. Then he started to get into more serious questions.

"Your sister mentioned on the phone you wanted to see me because you're struggling with an eating disorder?" he asked.

"Yeah, well, sort of," I told him. "She wanted me to see you. I kind of gave her a hard time about seeing a therapist. I didn't want to at first."

"So you do now?" he asked me.

I thought about it for a couple of seconds. I still didn't want to, but I didn't see any harm in it anymore.

"Yeah, I do. I think it could be beneficial," I told him.

"Well, what do you expect to get out of counseling?" he asked me. I didn't really know how to answer that question either. I sat in silence for a couple of seconds, trying to figure out what to say. "It's okay if you don't know. We can figure that out. Maybe by the end of this session," he told me.

"Let us talk about your family," he said. "Normally, when a minor's family member calls, it's one of their parents. Your sister called me. Is there a particular reason?"

I explained to him that my mother died and that my dad kicked me out shortly after. I didn't go into specifics on what happened the night he kicked me out; I didn't tell him that we got physical. I mentioned that I was an unplanned child, so my dad was always bad toward me.

"Now, at this point, were you already struggling with bulimia when this happened, or did this start after everything with your parents occurred?" he asked.

"I don't know how this fully developed, but I have to say that it probably started shortly after. Maybe even the week it happened," I told him. I could feel myself start to feel a little bad. Like tears were starting to build up.

"Do you think that everything that happened with your parents was one of the reasons this could have sta—"

"No," I said, shaking my mind. "As bad as everything is, I don't want my mother to be to blame for anything." A tear started to roll down my face as I started talking and thinking about my mother more.

"We aren't, Larry." He handed me a tissue. "No one gets blamed when this kind of stuff happens. But we do look at what triggers it. Like, think and answer me, do you think you'd be struggling with this if your mom didn't pass?" I thought about it for a couple of seconds.

"I don't know," I told him with the sound of uncertainty in my voice. "I'm not sure." We talked more about family for a little bit, about Blake and Emily and how helpful they'd been throughout all this. He asked me about other family members, and I didn't know anything to tell him. My dad had a few brothers that were just as bad of alcoholics as he was, and my mom had one sister that I hadn't seen since before my mom passed. Her husband died when I was young. I didn't remember him at all, but she and my mom were close.

"Why do you think your dad didn't want you around?" he asked. "There has to be a reason other than you were an 'unplanned child.'"

"His addiction," I said. "That's my only guess. When I was a little kid, I remember him being nice until he started drinking. After he started drinking, he just got verbally abusive toward me, and even sometimes my mom and sister. But even when he was sober, he was rude toward me. I guess he just couldn't see me through his eyes anymore? If that even makes any sense." He nodded in agreement and briefly explained what addiction does to the brain. The more we talked about my dad, the more it upset me. I think he could tell, and he moved on to a different subject.

"Do you have a girlfriend?" he asked. I briefly smiled. "There's a smile. How's Anna doing?"

I looked at him, puzzled for a second, and he started laughing.

"She and her family go to the same church I do. I know the family pretty well, so I heard about you before." He reminded me about the confidentiality laws and that everything I said about her here would stay here. We talked about her and our fight over me hiding everything from her. After that, he started asking me about my eating disorder.

"So what were your symptoms? What were you doing eating-disorder-wise?"

"I purge a lot, and I also try to just not eat in general, but that doesn't work. So that tends to lead to a binging-and-purging episode," I explained.

"When was the last episode you had?" he asked me, and I told him that I had one last night. He got a confused look on his face for a second and then continued.

"How much do you binge and purge?" he asked. "Currently."

"I don't keep track, but I'd say it's becoming an everyday thing. I go running a lot, too, to try to lose weight as well, hopefully, to burn off calories that I didn't get out earlier." He asked me again if I was currently doing that, and I said yeah. He got quiet for a couple of seconds. At this point, we had about twenty minutes left of our session. He closely leaned forward in his chair and put his notes down next to him.

"Larry, I've enjoyed talking to you. I will continue talking to you. But in my professional opinion, I think the next step in moving forward here is going into an inpatient program." The second he said that, my heart started beating quickly.

"What?" I asked him. "Like a rehab? For how long?"

"I wouldn't call it a rehab. It's just a treatment program to better help someone in your situation. It can be anywhere between a few weeks to a few months. I know a place in Princeton that you ca—"

"No way that's happening!" I yelled, standing up. "I hardly wanted to come here, let alone get locked up for a couple of months."

"Larry, this isn't anything to be scared of." He was still sitting down. "If you're actively hurting yourself with this disorder, then I don't know if can help you. If you get hurt in any way, then I can be held responsible for you. You need to go to inpatient. It's for your own good."

"I'm not freaking going. There is no way. You can't make me do it," I said.

"You're right, I can't. Only your legal guardian can," he said.

"Then who?" I asked "My dad? He doesn't give a crap about me! He won't make me go!"

"Please, Larry, just have a seat and try to remain calm. I'm sure we can figure something out."

"No, no, no way," I said. "I gave this a try, and it's not working. I'm leaving."

"Larry!" he called for me as I was walking toward the door. I turned around, and I looked at him. He told me, "You're not really mad at me. Deep down you know it's the best thing to do. If you go, or if you decide to go, please give me a call. I'll help you get in."

"Stop trying," I said through tears and stormed out the door, slamming it behind me.

I stormed out to my truck and slammed the door as I was getting in. I death-gripped the steering wheel and took a couple of seconds to breathe deeply and try to calm myself down. There was no way I was going to an inpatient program.

For him even to suggest that I was that unhealthy for him to talk to made me furious. I took a couple deeper breaths to calm myself down as well as I could. I looked at my phone and saw a text from Anna: "Call me after therapy and let me know how it goes!" I drove down the road and started to call her to tell her what happened.

"Hey, hun," I said. "I just got out of therapy."

"Hey, babe. How did it go?" she asked.

"Good at first. I ended up leaving early. He told me he suggests going to an inpatient program. I stormed out after that."

"You're not taking his advice?" she asked.

"No," I said. "I'm not. I don't need to. I can get better without inpatient. I'll just find another therapist to talk to." There was a moment of silence over the phone.

"Can we meet?" she asked. "I really want to see you."

"Yeah, of course!" I said. My day was starting to get better. "Do you want me to come over?" She told me yeah, and I told her I'd be right over, and we hung up. After that counseling session, seeing her was going to make my evening so much better. I started to speed up to get there faster. I could already feel my night getting better.

When I got to her house, her parents weren't home—at least their cars weren't there. Anna was already sitting on her front porch, waiting for me. I pulled up, and I was going to get out of the truck, but she walked over and got in the passenger side.

"Hey, babe," I said, and I went to go kiss her, but before I could, she started talking.

"This won't take long," she said. "I thought you said you were going to start being honest with me," she said. I sat back from the rejected kiss and felt confused.

"I am?" I said through my confusion.

"You told me that you didn't know where your dad was. That after your mom died, you had to move in with your sister. So why did Brandon tell me he kicked you out after your mom died?"

*Freaking Brandon,* I thought to myself. Before I could even answer, she started talking again.

"And now, when you know you're so sick that a counselor is telling you to go to treatment, you're taking it as bullcrap and not going? Are you insane?" She looked angry, even more angry then she sounded over the phone during our last argument. I sat not knowing what to say. I mean, sooner or later, she was going to find out about my dad; tonight was just not the time I wanted her to know.

"Anna, I don't need to go," I said. "I'll be fine without it."

"You're not fine!" she yelled. "You need to stop telling yourself that, because it's not true."

"Well, I don't want to go," I said. "And I'm sorry, but this is my decision to make. At least give me the night to think things over before I make any decision on this." She started tearing up.

"Larry, I can't do this," she said. "If you're not even healthy enough to take care of yourself, you sure aren't healthy enough for a relationship."

"What?" I asked. The moment she said that, I could feel my heart starting to shatter. "You don't mean that."

"Well, how can I love you when I hardly know you? Everything you told me about yourself so far is a lie," she told me.

"Look, I know I have my problems, but everyone does. This isn't something to end a relationship over."

"I'm sorry, Larry, and I know this is going to sound cruel, but I'm not dating someone who's not only a bulimic but also can't even be man enough to admit to themselves they have a problem. You need help. Be a man. You shouldn't even be struggling with this. This is normally a girl's problem."

My anger at that started to get higher than it was with Dr. Beech.

"Then go," I said.

"Anna!" I yelled, bottling up the tears I wanted to let out, tears that I probably should have let out. She turned around and looked at me. "Please don't go."

"Maybe when you're healthy, people can start to love you again," she said, and she walked back into her house.

I sat there for a couple of seconds. I started to bottle up any tears that I had and held on to them. I didn't want to let one drop over her. The second I got to the point where I could drive without focusing on holding tears in, I started to drive home. Her words kept playing back through my mind over and over.

*Maybe when you're healthy, people can start to love you again... Be a man. You shouldn't even be struggling with this... This is normally a girl's problem.* This wasn't just a problem for girls, I thought. It couldn't be. All the words she said and the feelings she just left me with raced through my mind to the point that the second I pulled into my driveway, I couldn't even get out of the car yet. I sat there and started crying. More tears poured out of me than when my mom passed. Everything started building up, and I didn't know what to do. I couldn't be mad at Brandon for telling her. I knew that much. I was the one that lied to her; he was just the one that told her the truth. I was sane enough to figure that one out. I went into the empty house, and for the first time since my dad threw me out, I felt completely alone in the world again, except this time I didn't even have my health.

I called Brandon.

"Hello?" he asked.

"Hey," I said. "Anna just broke up with me."

"I heard," he said. "Bro, I'm so sorry that happened. Especially with everything you're going through. I am so sorry."

"When did you find out?" I asked him.

"About twenty minutes ago," he said. "Anna told Lilly she was going to. Lilly told me right away."

"So I was the last to know then," I said, and I wiped my face with the sleeve of my hoodie. "That's nice. You know, she told me I couldn't be loved again until I got healthy."

"Well, then, forget about her!" Brandon yelled. "There's much better than her out there! I know that's hard to see right now, but she'll come around."

"Yeah," I said. I could hear the fake hope in my own voice. "I guess."

"Right now, though, we do need to focus on getting you healthy. I know you don't want to go to treatment. I'm not telling you to go, and I'm not telling you not to go. What I am asking, one bro to another, is that you at least think about it." I was silent for a few seconds before he spoke again. "Larry? Are you going to think about it?" he asked.

"Yeah, I will," I said. "Give me the night."

"Okay. Good deal. Do you need to come over? Do you need to talk?"

I told him I was going to be fine, but he knew I was lying. He said he was one phone call or text away if I needed him and we hung up. I knew he was just trying to be a good friend, and so far, he was the only one who had taken into consideration how I felt about going to an inpatient program. If my dad was the only one who could make me legally go, then I probably wouldn't have to go. I thought about it for a few seconds, and I thought that if I called him and asked him, if he said he wanted me to go, then I would. If the man who hated me enough to throw me out after my mom died was even telling me I should go, then I would go. I called him. I didn't want to hear his voice, but on the other hand, I did. He picked up the phone, and then he hung it up right away. *Figures,* I thought to myself. I started to tear up again, over my dad, over Anna. I went to my room and rolled into bed and cried into my pillow for yet another time. It wasn't the first time I cried into my pillow, and it wouldn't be the last time.

Dr. Beech called Emily shortly after I stormed out and told her what happened. He told her that things did seem to be going well until he recommended that I go to an inpatient program. Then we got into a little spat and I stormed out. He said it was no different from talking to someone who had a drug addiction; if they were active in their addiction, then he would tell them that they needed to seek further treatment than just talking with him. He said if someone were to overdose, then he could get held responsible for them. It was the same concept as me; I needed to go to inpatient.

Emily came into my room that night to discuss talking to me about going to treatment, and I told her that I didn't want to go. She kept pressing me, but I wouldn't budge on it. I told her that I called Dad to see if he would even talk to me about it, but he wouldn't even answer the phone. After that happened, it really pushed me to not want to go. After she left, Blake came in.

"You know, I wish I could say I know what you're going through, but I don't," he said and started to walk closer to me. "I wish I did, though, so I would have better words to say." He came over and sat on the bed next to me.

"Anna broke up with me too," I said.

"I'm sorry to hear that," he told me. "I know breakups aren't easy, but there are other girls out there. I know it's hard now, but things will get better. You just can't hold this as a reason to not get healthy, or things won't." I sat in silence.

"We both love you, Larry," he said. "We love you a lot, but we need to know that you're okay. You've been asked enough by the doctor and Emily enough to get treatment, so I won't press you. But just know that the decision is yours. But just know that this decision will affect how you live the rest of your life." He stood up and walked toward the door.

"I'm not your dad," he said. "Obviously, I'm not. But I'll be the closest thing to a dad for you if you need me to be." He walked out.

That night, it was a little after ten o'clock, and I was hoping to be asleep, but I couldn't. I sat up, thinking of Anna, treatment options, everything that I was told today. It was more than I could handle. In the other room, I could hear Emily crying as Blake was trying his best to comfort her. I could hear her crying, saying she didn't want me to die, that she didn't want me to go. Blake was agreeing with her and promising that they could figure everything out. I continued to sit in bed, trying my best to hold tears in. But hearing Emily cry the way she did pushed me more than anything else did. I threw my face into a pillow and started screaming.

"No! No! No!" I screamed, and I threw the pillow into the wall and started beating my fists on my mattress. I could feel my face turn beet red, and sweat started pouring from me. I continued beating my fists against the mattress, screaming profanity and letting tears roll from my face. I turned and picked up the nightstand that was next to my bed and threw it on the floor. The good thing was that it didn't break. Throwing it did tear the carpet a little bit. I fell to my knees on the floor and put my head on the floor and put my hands over my head and let out one last yell. I burned all my anger and energy out and lay on my back in bed and stared at the ceiling as more tears rolled from my face.

*Maybe when you're healthy, people can start to love you again.* Those words played through my mind again. I couldn't help but think to myself, *If I have to be healthy to be loved, then I don't want to be healthy.* I felt fat, unlovable, unwanted. I couldn't help but feel that if I were to die in my sleep tonight, I wouldn't care.

The next morning, I didn't know where to go, so I went where I should have gone a while ago: I went go visit my mom's grave. I took flowers and laid them at her headstone and stood over her grave, looking down at it. It was cold and windy. The clouds rolled over the December sky as I stood and looked at the flowers that were probably going to die over the night when the frost covered them. I still felt the hurt and pain from the night before. There were plenty of country songs I could think of that referred to the morning blues.

"I'm sorry I didn't come to the funeral," I said like she was right there as I was talking to her. "I…I couldn't face Dad. It's funny, really, thinking of it all. This started when you passed. All of it. I don't blame you for any of it. That would be unfair. But I would give anything to have you here with me while I'm going through it." I stood there for a few minutes, holding in tears. I kissed my hand and patted her headstone and headed back to my truck. It was cold, and I could feel my face freeze.

Depression started to kick in over the weeks. There were nights I couldn't sleep and other nights when I couldn't get enough sleep. I started having night terrors. I'd wake up and my heart was pounding. There were also times that I had difficulty breathing. Everything seemed lost, hopeless. I tried my best to binge and purge less. I managed to do that less, for Emily's sake, but I started taking laxatives as a form to lose weight. I explained to Emily that I did plan on getting help, but in my ways. I was slowly going to stop. But I knew that she didn't believe me, that it would not be that easy. The worst part of it all was, I think she lost hope in me. At that point, I think I lost hope in myself too.

    Despite Anna breaking up with me, it didn't feel as sad as I did over the few days that followed. I started to get over the breakup, though not in a happy way. It was a feeling that I just didn't feel anything. I distanced myself from my friends for the most part. I joked around with them in school and work, but when I got home, I didn't really talk to anyone through text. I hardly talked to my sister either. I used my eating disorder to cope with everything that happened, losing my mom, getting thrown out by my dad. I was using it to feel happy. But the happiness never came. Now, I was using it to fill an empty void I felt inside. Loneliness, depression. After Anna left and I got told the best option was inpatient, I felt like I came to the end of my rope. I was finished. All I wanted at that point was to feel happier.

# CHAPTER 13

For Christmas in 2017, we did things a little different than Thanksgiving. Because of my sister and Blake going over to my dad's house for Christmas dinner, they decided to have a Christmas party for their friends and their friends' family a little after Christmas. They didn't want me to be alone. Even though it was well after the holiday, they still wanted to celebrate with me, so they waited until the other holidays were over to throw a party, so they knew no one had plans. I worked extra hard that year to get both good presents. I got Blake a Flyers jersey; he was a big hockey fan. I got my sister a huge stuffed Tigger. She loved Winnie the Pooh growing up. I remembered her having her room filled with Tigger stuffed animals. I thought it would be funny to get her one this year. My first Christmas living with them. They invited some of their friends from work over to dinner with their families.

The house was filled with guests, my sister's and Blake's friends and their children. There was food everywhere. My sister and Blake spent the entire day cooking for this Christmas party they were having. I was sitting on the couch by myself, not wanting to eat, but I was listening to everyone talk, and Emily came over and sat next to me.

"Did you eat yet?" she asked.

"Not yet," I said. "I invited Brandon over, so I'm waiting for him to get here." As I said that, Brandon came in with a *Die Hard* Christmas sweater on.

"My dude!" he yelled. He came over and plopped on the couch next to me and threw his arm around me. Lilly came in following behind him. "Merry Christmas, brother." He handed me a gift.

"I have yours underneath the tree!" I said. "Make sure you don't forget it on the way out."

Emily stood up, with a smile on her face.

"You guys go grab some food," she said and walked off. Now, I don't know if it was from *It's a Wonderful Life* playing on the television or if it was from the Christmas music playing from the kitchen. Maybe it was even from being surrounded by a bunch of people I knew cared about me. But I felt happy for once since Anna left. I felt really happy.

Brandon tried singing along to Christmas songs as they came on the speaker, butchering it terribly. That didn't stop him from trying to, though; he came in screaming song lyrics in a scratchy and cracking voice. I and the other guests were laughing while Lilly laughed in slight embarrassment.

I was looking at all the food my sister made and felt nervous. Emily could tell and pulled me to the side.

"You go sit down. Tell me what type of food you want and I'll go make you a plate," I told her, and I went to sit down. Brandon came over with a huge plate and sat down next to me. Lilly followed with a plate of her own. He was humming and singing along with Mariah Carey's Christmas music, and he started rocking me back and forth until I lost all seriousness and started singing along with him.

"All I want this year for Christmas is you, babe." He looked at Lilly. "But if it's okay, I'm gonna have Larry for

New Year's." He started laughing, and I jokingly punched his arm. Emily came over and put the plate down in front of me.

"Thank you," I said. She rubbed my forehead and walked off.

"Make sure you eat all that," Brandon said. "You've gotten way skinnier." He looked concerned. In front of me were ham, mashed potatoes, some vegetables, and plenty of sides, like a salad, some cheese, and crackers. Things I did actually enjoy eating. I started eating it, and Brandon's face went from concerned to smiling. I was glad to see him happy. I started to eat my food, and we talked about the semester ending soon. Finally, Brandon looked at Lilly.

"You want to tell him already?"

I looked surprised. "Tell me what?" I asked.

"I was talking to Anna," Lilly said. "She was talking about how she misses you. She was also thinking of giving you a call to see if you wanted to try again."

I smiled. The night had started to get better, and if there was a chance of getting Anna back, I wanted to take it. I ate more until I realized my plate was empty. It was a normal-size plate; maybe it wouldn't hurt me too much if I purged?

"Excuse me," I said and stood up.

"Hey, man," Brandon said, standing up. "You just finished eating. Where are you going?"

"To piss?" I said. Brandon looked at me in disbelief. "Look, it's Christmas. Can you just let me be happy for the night? I promise I'm not doing anything in there," I lied, but he bought it. I went to the bathroom.

The second I got in there, I started chugging water from the bathroom sink to make myself feel even more full, hoping it would help make this more quickly, so I could get out before Brandon or my sister knew what I was doing. I started purging. It wasn't coming up very easily, so I started purging more, or trying to purge more, pressing harder, and some food came up with water, but not enough. I went back to the sink and drank more water and returned to the toilet and tried to purge more. It wasn't coming up easily, so I kept pushing, and finally, some came up, but not by itself. I felt relief at first until I looked at the hand that I was using to make myself vomit, which was covered with red liquid. *Is that blood?* I thought to myself and stood up quickly and started coughing. More blood came up with it. I started panicking and rushed out of the bathroom. I was coughing, and the pain was unreal. Brandon rushed over to me, and I held up my hand to him. He saw blood running down.

"I think I need help!" I yelled. I coughed more blood; I could see it fall onto my shirt. Everyone in the party started freaking out, wondering what was wrong with me.

"Oh my god!" Emily rushed over, and I fell to my knees. I could tell that blood was now coming out of my nose too. I was feeling light-headed again. Emily and Blake rushed over and tried to keep me on my feet, but I fell on my side.

"Larry!" I heard Emily scream at me. "Larry, please, someone get help!"

People were rushing around me. Things started to fade. Suddenly, I started to feel cold. "Larry! Someone call 911!" I heard someone yell.

*What's going on?* I thought to myself. I heard someone yell my name one more time, then everything went black.

# CHAPTER 14

Christmas was always my favorite day of the year. It wasn't even because of the gifts or celebrating the holiday. It was because I was surrounded by people I knew loved and cared about me. Everyone seemed to forget about their problems for the day and gathered and showed one another love.

It was weird waking up in a hospital right after a late Christmas party, though.

I woke up in a hospital bed. There were IVs in my arm again, and I had a neck brace on too. I could see from where they had to cut my shirt off that it was completely bloodstained My throat hurt horribly. I felt a lot of pain from where I fell again too. I woke to Emily holding my hand and Blake sitting across the room. Brandon had pushed two chairs together and was sleeping.

"Emily," I said very softly.

"Shh," she said. "Don't speak. You're all right." She turned and looked at Blake to go get the doctor and tell him I was awake, and he rushed out of the room.

"I remember what happened," I said. "Right up to passing out, I remember everything." Tears started flowing down my face, and I started coughing. Emily had tears in her eyes, too, and she wiped mine away before wiping her own face. I looked at the clock and saw it was 1:20 a.m. I leaned my head back and focused on breathing. It was a couple of minutes, but the doctor finally came in. It was Dr. Robbinson again.

"Hello, Mr. Larry!" he said, coming in. "You know, I normally don't do overnight, but I was asked to fill in so the other doctor could surprise his daughter for her birthday. When I saw you got admitted again, I wanted to come down and see you myself."

I smiled at him. When he started talking, Brandon woke up and sat up in his chair.

"Do you know what happened, Larry?" he asked. I shook my head no. He started talking again.

"You put so much pressure on your esophagus from purging that you tore it. Also, you were purging so much in a short period you popped a blood vessel in your face." There was a short period of silence as I thought this over. "Mr. Larry, you need to go to inpatient, immediately. If you don't get help for this, there's no telling what will happen to you."

"What about school? This is my senior year. I have a graduation, prom, a lot of events coming up I don't want to miss," I replied. I was just using another excuse on why I didn't want to go to inpatient.

"Larry, this is in my full professional medical opinion. If you do not go to inpatient treatment, and if you do not get help for this, you won't be alive to see your high school graduation. We can cross that bridge when we get there. But for now, if you don't get the help, you will die."

Hearing those words sent chills down my back. For the first time since any of this had started, I was scared. I was scared of what was going to happen to me, what my sister would do if I died. Everything in one night fell back on me again because of this.

"And, Larry, we took your height and weight while you were sleeping. You are six foot five, and as of right now, you're

132 pounds. You're severely underweight. To lose as much weight as you did, as fast as you did, you're lucky to even be alive right now." He looked at my sister and then back at me. "Look, I'm going to go to the break room and make a pot of coffee for everyone. I need you guys to talk this over." He left the room.

"I'm sorry, guys," I said. "I am so sorry."

"We don't need you to be sorry," Blake said. "We need you to be healthy. We need you here with us."

More tears started pouring down my face.

There was another knock on the door. It was a man, a bigger guy with black hair that was starting to gray. He had his hair pushed back. He had a goatee that was starting to gray. He was wearing blue jeans and a Philadelphia Eagles hoodie.

"Thank you for coming here at this hour, Pastor," Blake said and walked over and hugged him.

"It's no problem," he said, and he walked over to my bedside, patting Emily's shoulder, and she grabbed his hand for a couple of seconds.

"How are you doing, bud?" he said. "My name is Pastor John. I'm the led pastor over where Blake attends when he's off work."

I nodded at him. "I'm Larry," I told him. "Did I have tests or something done? Were the results that bad they called you in at 1:00 a.m.?" I asked jokingly, and we both started laughing a little bit.

"No," he said with a smile on his face. "Not that I know of. I was over at the party when you had that episode. When you fell, Blake explained to me what happened, and we prayed while you were out."

"The doctor said I'm lucky to be alive right now," I told him.

"Well, what do you think? Do you believe that it's just luck? Or do you believe someone is looking out for you?" he asked.

I gave a fake chuckle. "No disrespect, but after everything I've been through, it's hard to believe that someone is actually watching out for me, wouldn't you think?"

Emily and Blake stood up, and they and Brandon started heading for the door.

"We'll give you two some time," they said, and they walked out the door into the hallway.

Pastor John took a seat next to me. "Son, I understand what you're feeling. That pain, that hurt," he said. "Let me be the first to tell you that you don't have to face that alone. Someone is there to help you through it all."

I started tearing up.

"Well, where is he?" I said. "Where was he when crap hit the fan. When I had to repeatedly pick myself back up? Where was God when I needed Him most?" I could tell John, maybe not fully, sort of started to feel the pain that I was feeling. His eyes started to turn red.

"He was reaching out to you," he said. "Jesus loves you. Even if you don't feel it, He's reaching out His hand to pull you out of this mess. Right here, right now. Don't believe for one second that He ever left your side. That He ever abandoned you. I don't know what you've been through, but I do know this: God said He'd never leave you or forsake you. He hasn't, Larry. Not for one second."

The second I heard that, a wave of emotions and tears started to overflow me as I started thinking about the past ever since my mom died. When my mom died, He was the one that got me home safely that night. When Dad threw me out and it felt like my own parents didn't love me, He was the one that gave me a loving sister to take me in with no questions asked. When Anna left me, He was the one that gave me the best loving friends I could ask for that never stopped checking in on me. Most of all, every time I purged, no matter how deep of a hole I dug myself in with bulimia, God was the one that threw down a ladder for me to crawl out and go get help. For the first time, my eyes were opened to what I was doing to myself, and I started crying again.

"It's hard, isn't it?" he asked me. A tear rolled down his face. "Having to live with all this pain and regret? Having to carry it alone?"

"Yes! All I feel are regret and pain from everything I've done," I told him.

"You don't have to," he told me. "You never had to. Son, just give it to Jesus."

"How?" I asked. "How do I do that?" He grabbed my hand and looked at me.

"Do you accept Jesus Christ as Lord and Savior?" he asked.

"Yes!" I told him. "I want to, right now, I want to accept Him," I added.

"Do you believe that after praying the prayer we are about to pray, if you were to die, right here in this bed, you'll see Jesus?" he asked. I nodded. He grabbed my hand with both of his, and I threw my other hand over top of his.

"Let's pray, then," he said softly. He said a prayer over me, and as he said it, I felt everything I was holding in come out; it came out in tears and coughing, but I started to feel a peace that I hadn't felt in so long. I still felt physical pain, I still felt urges to vomit, even sitting in that bed, but I also started to feel a peace that I knew I didn't have to face it alone anymore.

He stood up after praying and said, "What I prayed over you was Psalm chapter 51. It's a sinner's prayer. When you get a Bible, I suggest you read it again for yourself. I'll go get your family." He turned around, but I reached out and grabbed his hand and he turned around and looked at me.

"Thank you," I said through tears.

He smiled at me. "Welcome to the family," he said, and he walked out of the room and grabbed them.

When they came back in, Emily sat at my bed and Blake sat in his spot, with Brandon across the room again.

"I think I'm a Christian now," I told them. "I'm not too sure how that all works, but I'm excited to see where it goes."

"That's wonderful!" Blake said. He had a huge smile on his face that I had never seen before.

Dr. Robbinson came back in with a pot of coffee and a pack of cookies for everyone. He set them down and looked at me.

"Has everyone talked it over?" he asked.

"I'm ready to go to the inpatient program," I said. "What are the next steps?"

He looked shocked, and I didn't blame him. I was shocked hearing myself say it. I knew waking up in a hospital on Christmas wasn't what I was planning, but it was what I needed to do. For the first time, I knew and accepted that if I didn't make a change, I was going to die. There wasn't any way around it. I stayed for the rest of the night in the hospital and got discharged early the next morning.

When we got back to the house, we opened the presents we got from one another. I forced some food down on top of that. I had to start taking medications to prevent the tear in my esophagus from getting infected. I wasn't ready to die; I wasn't ready to give up.

I wish I could say from the moment I got out of the hospital to the moment I went to treatment, I learned my lesson and I didn't purge, and I didn't do anything to harm myself. But my story isn't a fairy tale. Things weren't perfect, and I still had struggles. I never heard from Anna and never got the call. Maybe when she heard I got put in the hospital again, she changed her mind. That was the least of my problems right now, though. I had to focus on getting healthy again, and I planned on just that.

When my sister called the inpatient program I was going to, they said it was going to be a couple of days before a bed opened, so for the meantime, I started praying. I started talking with Pastor John more about the Bible and what it means for us. I still purged and starved myself, unfortunately. I really struggled not to, but I failed a lot in those couple of weeks. My weight stayed the same during the next couple of days. I still harmed my body enough, even altering getting out of the hospital to keep my weight down. That was probably my biggest regret.

The night before I went into treatment, my sister came into my room while I was packing a bag.

"Hey," she said. "I got you something." She handed me a wrapped gift. When I opened it, I saw that it was a brand-new leather Bible with my name stitched on the cover. I smiled at it.

"Thank you," I said, and I hugged her.

"Do you have everything you need?" she asked.

"Yeah, I got everything. Everything I think they'll let me bring. What time should we leave tomorrow?"

"Around 9:00 a.m.," she said. "I'm going to head to bed," she said, and she turned around.

"I love you," I said. "Thanks for not giving up on me."

"I love you too," she said. "I never would." She walked out.

God gave me a new beginning, and inpatient would give me a new start. It was time to take it. Just breathe, live, and pray. Breathe, live, and pray.

Breathe…

Live…

Pray…

# CHAPTER 15

The morning I got ready to go to treatment was one of the scariest mornings I went through. I woke up lying in bed, staring at the ceiling. My bags were already packed from the morning before. I couldn't sleep. I wasn't even on my way there yet, and already I felt nervous about going, what to expect, how long I'd be there, and even the thought of just being away from home in general made me nervous. I doubted my dad even knew I was going. I had woken up before my alarm went off, so I was lying in bed, waiting for it to buzz and echo into my quiet room, when I started to hear Brandon's voice in the living room. I knew he was coming to ride up with us to Princeton, but I didn't expect him this early. He opened my bedroom door and yelled into my room.

"Wake that behind up, boy!" he started yelling while flickering my lights on and off. I started laughing. It was too early for him to be this energized. I'd been up for almost an hour, lying in bed, and I wasn't even that energized. I started to get out of bed. I was still in my boxers and T-shirt.

"I'll let you get ready," he said. "When you get done, meet me outside. Let's have a drink before we get going." He walked out of my room back out to the living room.

I got out of bed, shaved my face, and got a shower as fast as I could. *My guess is they probably won't allow me to have blade razors,* I thought to myself. Emily, who was already ahead of the game, bought me an electric razor and packed it in my belongings last night. I stood in the mirror, looking at my reflection. I couldn't recognize myself anymore. I didn't like who I saw. I didn't know who I was looking at, but it wasn't me. Before I could give my chance to get emotional, I turned out the bathroom lights and headed back to my room to get my bags and bring them out to the car.

"I never thought this would happen," I said. "Not me."

I was sitting on a curb outside Emily's house. My legs were crossed, one hand sitting on my lap while the other was on a zero-calorie Monster Energy. I didn't sleep well the night before, so I needed all the energy I could get. I looked down at my hands. They were already pale, and the bright morning sun shining on them made them look even worse. It was to the point where not only could I see the veins in them but I could also see the blue color coming through.

Brandon sat next to me, sipping his energy drink, looking forward toward the sun as it was still rising. Stubble hung from his face from not shaving when he got up in the morning. He woke up early to ride up to Princeton with Emily and me. I couldn't have asked for a better friend than him.

"You know, I joke around a lot, but I know this is going to be hard," he said, and he turned and looked at me. "Larry, this is going to be a really hard journey for you. Anyway, I'm proud of you for starting it." I was still looking down at my hands, and I began to smile. My face was cold from the winter air hitting my freshly shaved face.

"How did we get here?" I asked, looking up. "It feels like just yesterday we were playing Xbox in my room while my mom was downstairs, heating pizza rolls for us." I took a sip of my Monster and set it back down.

"Remember the time in choir when Tanner tripped and fell into you and gave you a bloody nose?" he asked. I started laughing. We sat on the curb for almost an hour, reliving the good times we had in school and growing up together. I didn't know how long I'd be gone, but I knew I was going to miss Brandon while I was.

"In all seriousness," he said, "you've recently decided to leave your current path and follow Jesus. I know I'm not the most religious person—shoot, I could probably stand to pay attention more on Sunday mornings—but I know how much this can help. Learn to lean on Him through everything."

I nodded in agreement.

"I know it's hard to abandon your path and follow a different one. Especially when you feel like it's the only one you have. I'm proud of you, bro," he said, smiling. When he said that, it sent chills down my back. He was right; I was going to try to leave my path and follow Jesus down a new one. I just needed help getting on the new one.

"I appreciate you coming," I said. "I could use all the support I could get."

"That's what she said," Brandon said under his breath. He turned his head to me and smiled while setting his energy drink on the curb. He put his hand on my shoulder and started shaking me back and forth.

"We're going to get through this," he said. "We're brothers. We've made it this far. We're going to make it a lot farther." I could tell he was upset. I could hear him forcing words up, and he was trying to cover it up with jokes, but I knew how he felt.

The drive there, I was mostly quiet. Emily drove while I rode shotgun, and Brandon was in the back. I had no idea what this rehab program would be like, or even what it looked like. I knew it was a unit in a hospital, though, which gave me a negative picture of what the place would be like. I pictured that there would be monitors everywhere, cameras in every corner. I was worried the staff wouldn't be too friendly, maybe fed up with their job and what they had to put up with, so they took their frustration out on patients. I hated hospitals; I hated the thought of one. How could I focus on recovery with nurses constantly breathing down my back and the sound of monitors beeping? What also bothered me was the thought of what the other patients would be like. If they would be friendly and easy to get along with?

The hospital was over two hours away from my home as well, which I didn't like. Not only would I be in a hospital and a rehab, but I would also be far from home. Far from what I knew, my friends, my sister. The positive part was, I'd be far from my dad.

"Does Dad know where I'm going?" I asked Emily. "Did you ever tell him?"

"I did last night," she said. "He didn't say much about it. I didn't tell him what you were being hospitalized for. Just that you were being hospitalized."

The closer we got, the more nervous I started to feel. I could already picture in my mind a square flat-roofed stone hospital that looked more like a jail than a medical clinic. With a staff that was ruder than correctional officers. But when we finally got there, I saw something completely different.

Princeton Health Medical Care was the name of the facility I was going to. When we pulled in the parking lot, the scary-looking building turned out to be beautiful. From the outside, it appeared to be six floors but extremely long horizontally. It had a pond with a fountain inside of it in front of the building. The front of the building was made with mostly windows. I was shocked to see how beautiful the building looked compared to what I thought it was going to. It looked more like an upscale hotel than a hospital.

"This is the place?" I asked in confusion.

"Yeah, it should be," Emily replied. I sat in awe looking at the building. It was mesmerizing. If the inside looked as nice as the outside did, maybe it wouldn't be as scary as I thought.

"I'll grab your bags," Brandon said as we parked the car. I didn't bring much. Their website said they allowed us to have our cell phones during certain hours of the day, so I assumed we couldn't be able to have much technology besides that. I only packed one week's worth of clothes, hygiene products, and the electric razor Emily bought me. Despite the building looking better than I expected, I still was nervous as we approached the lobby. My stomach was in knots. Emily could tell and locked her arm with mine as Brandon followed behind us with the two small bags that I had packed. It was freezing outside, but the second we walked into the building, the heat hit my face and I saw that the inside of the building looked as beautiful as it did on the outside. Shiny white floors with tan-colored walls. It had a gift shop you could see as you came in, and a shop for cancer patients to buy wigs. The second you walked, you saw a sign that had the layout of the first floor. It had it all. An art gallery, chapel, cafeteria for guests and employees. It was beautiful. Not knowing where to go or where the eating disorder treatment part of the building was, I walked and approached the secretary sitting behind the front desk.

"Hello," I said in a quieter voice. I was still in awe of the building. "I'm here because I have an appointment to get admitted for bulimia."

The woman behind the desk was beautiful as well, couldn't have been older than her young twenties.

"Of course," she said, smiling. She pointed to my right. "You follow that hall and it will take you to the elevators. You want to go up to the fifth floor. It's the unit on the west side of the building."

"Thank you, ma'am," Emily said. She started walking toward the hall, and I followed behind with Brandon.

"Not bad," Brandon said. I nodded in agreement. "Not just the girl behind the counter, but this building too."

"Stop," I said, laughing, and pushed him to the side. He laughed and shoved into me with his shoulder.

When we got out of the elevator, I saw it had a mini lobby on its own. No front desk or anything, just a sitting area. The wall on the front of the building was entirely made of glass, so you could sit and see a beautiful view from five stories up. It looked like there were only two units on the fifth floor too. The eating disorder area took the entire west side of the fifth floor. We approached the doors to the building, and right away my heart felt like it dropped into my stomach. There was a sign on the door, in friendly colors:

*For entry, please press the button to the side. Welcome to Six North!*

With that, it had an arrow pointing to the button on the wall.

"Six North?" I asked, a little lost on what they meant. It took me a few seconds for it to click that it meant the north side of the sixth floor. Nevertheless, when I pushed the button, someone answered almost instantly.

"How can I help you?" a female voice answered through the speaker.

"Uh, yeah," I said. I sounded as nervous as I felt. "My name is Larry. I'm here to get admitted."

"Certainly!" she said back in a happy and exciting voice. At least one of us felt excited about this. "Take a seat out in the lobby and someone will be out with you shortly." I turned and went out to the sitting area and rested on one of the chairs while Brandon stood with his back to me, looking out the window. Emily sat in the chair across from me.

"This is it," Brandon said. "This is really happening." I puffed air through my nose and shook my head. I was still surprised I was here; I couldn't imagine how they felt. He turned and faced me and Emily.

"When you're here," Emily said, "don't just go through the motion. Really give this your all at getting better. We need you to get better. This is a time you can really sit and reflect on not only everything you've been through but also reflect on what God has for you." I didn't know what to say or if I should have said anything; I just smiled.

"And if you need anything, if you need to talk bro to bro, because you want guy talk, you know you can always call me," Brandon assured me.

"If I'm even allowed to have my phone on me," I added. He just met my comment with a smile. Around that time, an older gentleman came out with a woman next to him.

"Hello!" the woman exclaimed. "You must be Larry." She reached out her hand to shake mine. I shook her hand, then shook the hand of the man standing next to her.

"My name is Diane," the woman said. "I am the director of the eating disorder unit here. This is Dr. Smith." She pointed at him. Right off the bat, I could tell I was wrong about how the staff was going to be too. I expected the staff to be miserable, but Dr. Smith and Diane both greeted me with smiles and, from first impressions, seemed like happy and friendly people.

"Larry, if you could come with me," Dr. Smith asked. He had a thick Southern accent. "We have a few things to go over. You two can stay out here with Ms. Diane, and we'll come back for you." I followed Dr. Smith through the threshold of the door. *I'm officially a patient. Let's give life another try.* I walked into the unit with a pounding heart and nothing to lose.

The very moment we walked into a unit, we walked into a door on the wall next to the entrance and into an office. There was just a nurse who was in here, waiting for us.

"Okay, Larry, take a seat for me. Before we admit you, I just need to go over basic information with you," Dr. Smith said. He introduced me to the nurse, whose name was Lilly. He just asked the information he probably already had. My full name, age, date of birth. I confirmed all the information he had on his computer. He then asked if I was taking any medications, how my mood was. He asked if I felt sad, had any thoughts on harming myself, and I assured him that I didn't.

"Okay, Larry," he said. "Now, what symptoms of eating disorders do you have?" I sat silently for a few moments. Even though he was a doctor, this was hard for me to admit.

"I purge, and recently I started taking laxatives," I said. "I over-exercise sometimes, too, when I go running."

"Do you restrict at all?" he asked in a softer voice. I looked at him with a confused gaze. "Skip meals. Things like that," he specified for me. I nodded. I felt so ashamed I didn't even want to say the words. He started to ask more questions to follow up with those, like how often I did it. He then went on to ask if I had any other addictions I wasn't telling anyone about. I didn't. Besides drinking at Brandon's party a while back, I hadn't drunk at all in my entire life. We talked for a little while about my hobbies. I guess he was trying to get my mind on better subjects than the eating disorder. Overall, I thought he was a nice guy from the start. He had black hair he combed and gelled back. He was shorter but heavier set. The entire time we talked, Nurse Lilly sat in silence.

"Okay, well, before we get you admitted, I want to go over how our program works. Does that sound good?" he asked. I nodded. It sounded as good as it was going to get.

"Every patient here becomes a member of a team. A team consists of the patient, a psychiatrist, which for your team will be me, a nutritionist, and a therapist. You will meet with me and your therapist every day during the week, and you'll meet with your nutritionist twice a week. On Fridays we will all get together and discuss your process. Sound good?" he asked.

"Yes, sir. I mean, Doctor," I said.

He laughed and shook his head. "Let's get you admitted, bud," he said.

We walked out of the office and went down the hall to an open area labeled the "nurses' station." Across the hall from the nursing station was a room with a TV and few people in it that looked my age. I couldn't help but notice one of the girls. She was wearing a red shirt; she had a nose piercing and long dirty-blond hair. She looked beautiful.

"That's the adolescent group room," Dr. Smith said. I turned my focus back to him. We walked into a medical examination room, where they took my height and weight. They wouldn't tell me what my weight was; they said they only discussed numbers like that on Wednesday, during the meetings with our psychiatrist. After that, they made me take my shirt and jeans off and examined my body for any form of self-harm. The whole thing was making me feel uncomfortable and sad. *I shouldn't have to be here,* I thought to myself. I should be in school, joking around with my friends. I should be getting ready for college. The fact that I had to be in treatment and had to have my body examined the way it did made me feel worse. After I got fully dressed again, they took some blood and took me back to the office, where Emily and Brandon were waiting with Diane.

"Okay," Dr. Smith said when we got back to the office. "I'm going to leave you here with Diane. She'll take care of you from here." He smiled and shook my hand.

"I'm looking forward to working with you," I said. I wasn't fully lying. I was looking forward to working with him, just not why I did.

"You too." He smiled and left.

"How long do you expect Larry to be here?" Emily asked almost instantly.

"It really depends on him," she said. "I've seen patients here for a couple of weeks to a few months. It all depends on how he does while he's with us. I can assure you, though, while he is with us, he'll be the best care we can give him." I didn't know what she meant by that or what "How I do" was supposed to mean. Diane went over what Dr. Smith and I went over, about my team and how the program worked. She then discussed that visitor times would be from six thirty to nine forty-five. Cell phone time was from after dinner until nine forty-five, and bedtime was at ten, with an additional hour on the weekends. With that, I signed paperwork and Emily signed paperwork as well, because as a seventeen-year-old, I couldn't do it myself.

"Okay," Diane said. "Now, I'll take your bags to the storage closet while we go through them. I'll also need your cell phone," she said, holding her hand out. I took it out of my pocket and gave it to her, and she stood up.

"I'll give you a couple of moments to talk before we get started, Larry," she said, and she walked out of the room, leaving us alone. I sat for a couple of minutes in silence. Emily next to me. Brandon sat by the door of the office.

"I guess it's too late to back out now," I said and gave a chuckle filled with false hope. Emily reached across the table and grabbed my hand with her. Tears filled her eyes.

"I'm proud of you," she said, her voice cracking. I looked down at my lap. I didn't know what to tell her. I knew I had to be here. I just couldn't get over the feeling of not wanting.

"Now, when you get out," Brandon said as he was standing up and coming over to sit at the table, "we can have a party and celebrate. But for now, we need you to get better." I smiled. He continued talking. I stood up, and Emily hugged me.

"I know you can overcome this," she whispered through her tears. "We'll visit as often as we can. You can call me during your cell phone hours on days we can't."

"I'm going to blow your phone up if you don't," Brandon said, laughing. I couldn't help but laugh with him.

"Get well, bro," he said as he came over and threw his arms around me as well. *Don't cry,* I thought to myself. *Not here.* It was my first time having to go through something like this. I had to look strong. I didn't know if I had to look strong for myself or them, though. Brandon opened the door, and they walked out. I stood in an empty room for a couple of moments, alone. As I stood there in that office by myself, I knew day 1 of my life was going to take place; I just couldn't help but feel I was in it by myself as the ones I loved the most walked out of it. Diane poked her head back into the room and smiled as she walked in.

"I know day 1 is hard," she said. "Trust me, I know it is. Is this your first time in a program like this? An inpatient one, I mean."

"Yes, ma'am," I said in a soft voice.

"As you move through the program, I promise it'll get easier. Right now, you probably feel alone and nervous about starting, but the more you work on yourself and the more you push, the faster it'll go away, I promise," she assured me. "Come on, let me show you around the unit and introduce you to some of the staff."

Diane took me back to the entrance of the unit and began to show me the layout of the building. The second I walked into the eating disorder unit, I saw a little map on the wall that gave the layout of the unit. It was literally just a rectangle. When I walked into the entrance of the unit, I could go into a medical room the second I walked in, or I could walk straight down the hall. Like with most hospitals, as I walked down the hall, I noticed it was lined with bedrooms for the patients. About halfway down the first hall was the group room for adolescents.

"I know you're seventeen, and to be honest, you're closer to some of the young adults' age, but you're still an adolescent, so you must do all your group activities in this group room, okay?" Diane told me.

"Oh yeah, I fully understand," I said. She took me inside the adolescent room and showed me. There were a couple of couches, a table, and a huge flat screen with an Xbox connected to it. I was looking at the TV when another patient came in.

"Hello!" she said, walking in.

"Sarah!" Diane said. "I want you to meet Larry. He's a new adolescent guest."

Sarah shook my hand and smiled. "Finally, another adolescent."

I shook her hand, and we introduced each other.

"We can catch up with her later," Diane said. "Come on, Larry. I'll show you the rest of the unit."

Across the hall from the adolescents' group room was a nursing station and a room for patients to take their medication. We kept going straight down the hall, though, and then there were more bedrooms, then when we got down to the end of the hall, it took a right and there was the dining hall, which had two tables in there. A man was cleaning them as we walked past them.

"That's Matt," Diane said. "We can meet him in a bit. He's one of our wellness couches here. He works with us during the week."

When we passed the dining hall, we made another right, and it was a second hallway. It was lined with rooms, too, but the only difference in this hall was that there was the adult group room, and across from the adult group room was the nursing station again. So we could walk from the adult group room, through the nursing station, and get to the adolescent group room. As I said, the unit was one big rectangle. When we got close to the end of the second hallway, we stopped and walked into a bedroom.

"This will be your room," she said. "Go on in and look around. That's all I got for you now. Lunch will be served in about an hour. So feel free to explore the unit more. Go back to the group room. Make yourself comfortable if you like. Just don't do too many laps around the unit."

"Understood," I said, and I turned. I looked at her. "Thank you so much."

"No problem, sweets," she said with a smile on her face, and she walked out.

My new room was simple. A bed, a bathroom that, of course, was locked. There was a giant window with curtains over it I could open if I wanted. There was also a desk and a closet with a dress next to it. I opened the curtains, which overlooked what was behind the hospital. A large parking lot with scattered trees. Farther out, outside the hospital's property, was nothing but woods for the most part, but in the distance, I could see a church steeple. It was made of brick. The church was old, from what I could tell, like from an old-time movie. I wished I could be there.

My room felt like home, as it could possibly be; instead of white walls that screamed *hospital*, they were teal. The woodwork on the doors was impressive. The only thing that made it look any different from a normal bedroom was the hospital bed. I didn't have much to do; they had my bags, which had my Bible in it, and my phone was gone. I didn't fully feel comfortable talking to any of the other patients yet, so I got in bed and tried to make myself comfortable.

I had to admit, I didn't think I was going to make it during my first day. I knew if I wanted to complete this program, there was going to be a lot of hard work involved. I was going to have to make strong sacrifices, and I didn't know If I would be able to. I looked up at the ceiling of my room. Pale white, it somewhat matched with the lime-green-tiled floors of my bedroom and the hallway. I closed my eyes and tried to spend the next hour asleep.

"Lunchtime! Please come down to the dining hall!" a loud voice came over the speaker and woke me up. It scared me awake, and I almost fell out of the bed. I didn't notice at first, but next to my bed was a speaker built into the wall. It had a couple of buttons on it. One said "Push for emergency," and another button said "Push for bathroom unlock." I stood up for a couple of seconds to try to calm down, and then I walked down to the dining hall. I walked, and other patients were walking with me, but I was so nervous I didn't say anything to them besides my name when a couple of them asked. At the end of the dining hall was a cart that had everyone's tray on it. It had our name put on the end of it. I grabbed the tray that was mine. There were two tables. I didn't know which one to sit at, so I went to sit down next to another male patient and looked at my tray. A burger, a side salad, a yogurt, and a Coke.

I sat there for a couple of minutes, just looking at my tray. I said a quick grace in my head and just looked at it. I knew I had to eat it, but what was more nerve-wracking for me wasn't that I had to eat it but that once I did, there would be no way I'd be able to get it back up. I wouldn't be able to exercise much either. The nurses didn't even want us walking around the unit too much. My heart started racing, and I balled my hands up into fists. I felt like I was about to get emotional. *You can do this,* I thought to myself. *You can do this, you can do this, you can—*

"Are you okay?" the guy sitting next to me asked. I looked over at him, and he had a concerned smile on his face.

"Blessed and highly favored," I told him. I looked back at my food.

"We've all been there. First meal on the first day here. I know it's tough, believe me," he said while slowly eating the food on his plate. "My name is Dean."

"Larry," I said, and I quickly turned and shook his hand. I turned back to my food and picked up my burger and took my first bite. After swallowing the food, I took a deep breath before taking another. I tried my best to remain calm. I didn't know what punishments there were to skipping meals yet, or if there were any to begin with. Truth be told, I didn't want to find out.

"I have to say, this place is going to make you mad. There are times when this place is fun and other times it's completely painful and you'll wish you weren't here. But overall, the program has helped me a lot so far. I've only been here a couple of weeks, but I seem to have the gist of it," he told me. Dean had short black hair and some stubby facial hair. He was just wearing a thick white T-shirt and blue jeans. He seemed more built but was shorter than me.

"The best thing to do if you want to get out of here quickly," he explained, "just eat your meals and gain the weight they want you to. They discharge people here for their weight, which honestly is bull, because we have eating disorders, not weight disorders. But it is what it is."

I started to eat more, then I looked at the other table across the room. Sarah was sitting there with a younger boy and a second girl. Just the three of them sitting alone while the table Dean and I were at had over twenty people.

"Larry!" Diane walked into the room. "I apologize, I forgot to tell you, this table is for the adults. You need to sit at the other table with the adolescents."

"You're a minor?" Dean looked confused. I did look a little bit older than my age.

"I'm seventeen," I said, chuckling. He smiled at me and chuckled a little too.

"Well, we can catch up later on," he said. "Hey, why don't you swing by my room later and we can chat if you want?"

"I'm looking forward to it!" I said, standing up. I grabbed my tray and walked over to the adolescent table as the nurses monitoring us while we ate apologized for not realizing how old I was.

"What's going on, folks?" I said, sitting down.

"Bone app the teeth," the younger boy said.

"What?" I asked.

"We're coming up with funny ways to say *bon appétit*," Sarah said, laughing. "Zach here is dead set on 'bone app the teeth.' I'm going with 'boneless feet.'" She started laughing again. I smiled and took another bite out of my food and listened to the three of them go back and forth for a couple of minutes until the boy talked to me.

"What's your name, new guy?" he asked me. I told him my name, and he said his name was Zach. The girl sitting across from Sarah introduced herself as Bethany.

"Your turn, Larry," Zach said. "What's your way of saying it?"

I thought for a couple of seconds. "Bob ate the beef?" I said, questioning myself.

Zach still chuckled at it and went with it. The more we talked about it and laughed, the more I had bites of my food without noticing. They did a good job keeping my mind off it. When I looked down at my plate, I realized that I only had a few bites of my salad left and my Coke. I managed to eat my entire burger and most of the salad without realizing it. The second I realized I did, though, I started to feel nervous again. I turned my attention back on the three people as fast as I could. *Don't focus on the food,* I kept telling myself. After thirty minutes, people started raising their hands. Nurses came out and one by one started looking through the trays of the adults.

"What's going on?" I asked in a whisper to Sarah.

"We get forty-five minutes for lunch," she whispered back. "After thirty minutes, though, if you're finished you can raise your hand. Nurses go through your tray, though, to make sure you're not hiding food anywhere."

I looked at my Coke; I didn't even open it yet.

"You can save that for a snack," she said. "You can save three items from meals and eat them for snacks later if you choose to. But they must be eaten by the end of the day."

I shook my head. I raised my hand with the rest of the group at my table. A nurse came and looked through my empty tray.

"Good job, Larry," the nurse said. She looked down at me with a big grin and wrote my name in Sharpie on the can of Coke.

"What now?" I asked.

Sarah stood up. "We got about forty minutes until our next group," she explained. "So now we get to go hang out in the group room."

I went to go use the bathroom before meeting them in the group room, and it was one of the most awkward experiences I ever had. Of course, the bathroom in my bedroom was locked. I had to ask a nurse if she could unlock it for me. She walked me to my bathroom and handed me a plastic tube.

"What's this for?" I asked.

"When you go into the bathroom, I need you to pee in this," she said. I looked puzzled at her for a second.

"Since you're new here, you're on what we call bathroom observation. We have to watch you go to the bathroom, and when you go, we have to look and see what it looks like." I felt awkward just hearing her say that. I went into the bathroom and closed the door behind me, but the nurse right away cracked it back open.

"Please remember to keep it open just a crack. We need to be able to hear what you're doing in there."

My eyes opened up wide; it was my first day, and their rules were already annoying me.

The bathroom was small, and the toilet didn't have a handle on it to flush it. There was a button on the wall to flush it that required some sort of key to reach. It felt weird, but I doubt this type of experience is any more fun for the nurse.

I walked out of the bathroom, and she went in to look. I rushed out of the room before she even had a chance to look at anything. I started to walk quickly to the group room. The more I thought about it, the more it seemed funny to me. Then when I finally got into the group room, I had an awkward grin on my face. Zach was playing the Xbox, while Bethany and Sarah were sitting on the couch. I walked in, and right away Sarah looked at me.

"I've seen that look before," Sarah said and started smiling. "They introduced you to bathroom obs, didn't they?" I walked in and sat down on a love seat that was against the wall when I walked in. The whole wall that connected the group room to the hallway was made of glass, I guess so the staff could see inside of the group room.

"Big-time," I told her. "I knew using the bathroom would be different here, but I didn't know it would be that bad."

"It gets better," Zach said. His full focus was on the TV. It looked like he was playing Minecraft. "You'll be on it for about a week and a half or two weeks. It really depends on what eating disorder you're here for. Which in my opinion is a stupid way to look at it. But after that, they'll unlock the door and leave while you use it. They'll even leave it unlocked overnight."

"Well, how long have you been here?" I asked him.

"Ten weeks," he told me. "I should be going home a week from today."

I felt as if my heart skipped a beat when I heard that. *Ten weeks…I could be here for ten weeks…maybe even longer.*

"I got here two days ago," Sarah said. "This isn't my first time here, though." When she said that, I could hear that she sounded ashamed of herself.

"Bethany here goes home in a couple of hours!" She started patting her on the back. "And we are so proud of her."

Bethany smiled.

The more I looked at the TV and what Zach was making in Minecraft, the more it looked like he was building the facility. It looked really accurate too. From what I'd seen of it, it looked like he made the entire unit we were in. I kept trying to focus on that and less on the fact that I'd possibly be here for months. I sat back and took some deep breaths. Sarah came over and pulled up a chair next to mine.

"I can tell you're nervous," she said. "Trust me, I know this place probably isn't where you want to be for longer than, well, a minute, but I promise you, it's not as bad as you think. You'll make friends and we'll push through it. All right? We'll probably get out around the same time." I smiled and shook my head and really got a better look at her. She was beautiful. She had long dirty-blond hair and bright-green eyes. I didn't know why, but I felt comfortable when I was around her.

Diane came into the room.

"Group time," she said. "You can either go down to the chapel or you can go to the kitchen for arts."

Sarah stood up. "I'm going to arts," she said. "You coming?" she asked.

"That's what she said," Zach said, walking us, making his way to the kitchen. Diane started following him to talk to him about making those types of jokes. But he was just a young teenager. What more could you expect from him?

"I would, but I think I should go to the chapel," I said.

"You're a Christian?" she asked.

"Yeah," I said. "I'm very new to the faith, but I am."

She smiled at me. "I wish I could believe in that kind of stuff, but I don't," she said. "That's cool that you do. My boyfriend does too."

*She has a boyfriend,* I thought to myself.

She started laughing. "You look so confused, like you don't know what to say," Sarah said while laughing. "It's fine. Go to chapel. I'll see you later," she said, and she started walking away. She walked toward the dining area, and I turned and walked toward the entrance of the unit to meet a group of people. All adults. A couple of nursing staff came over to escort us down.

"Is everyone who's going here?" Diane asked. Kind of weird she'd ask that since if someone who was going wasn't here, they couldn't answer that question.

"Let's go!" she said.

"Hey, Larry," Dean said as we started walking down.

"Hey, man," I said.

He patted me on the shoulder. "Your first group here and it's chapel," he said. "You're going to like it. To be honest, it's one of the more relaxing groups of the week. There's no service. They just take us down and let us do whatever we feel we need to. Pray, read, have a Bible study. Any form of religious practice."

"Is there any way I could at least speak with a pastor or someone?" I asked.

"Sure," he said. "I don't see why not. Just ask Diane before we go in. They just escort us down and then wait outside. They give us forty minutes."

When we got to the doors of the chapel, I told Diane that if she could let me, I'd like to speak with a chaplain, and she told me she'd go get one out of their office for me. I walked into the chapel, and the first thing I noticed was how big it was. It was like a church was sitting inside of a building. It had pews, the altar, everything you'd see in a normal church. It just amazed me that this facility had everything.

I sat down in the second pew and looked up at the cross hanging over the altar. Everyone was spread out to pray. Everyone found their own pew or seat and was either praying or reading their Bible or Tanakh. I sat up, looking at the cross. I was stumped for words; I was trying to figure out what to pray and how to pray it. What words to tell God before I fully started other groups and treatment.

*God, I don't know where to go from here, but please show me what to do.* I sat in silence, not knowing what to say. I felt sad. I started thinking of home. I was hours away, stuck in a place I didn't want to be in, but I knew I had to be here. I hated myself for it. I hated that I needed to get help for something I thought I could control. Tears started to fight their way from my eyes, and I was doing my best to hold them in when a man came and sat next to me. He was bald but had brown facial hair. He was wearing all black, too, with a white collar. It was a priest.

"I'm sorry to interrupt," he said in a quieter voice. "I was told by someone that you requested to see a chaplain. You're new here, though, aren't you? I haven't seen you before."

"Yeah," I said. "I'm new here. It's my first day."

"My name is Bill. I'm one of the head chaplains here."

"Larry," I replied. "My name is Larry."

"Well, Larry," he said, "I must admit, seeing you from across the chapel, I noticed you looked a little down. Sort of lost too. Is there something on your mind? Something I can pray over you for?"

"I'm not Catholic," I told him. "I'm not sure if the way I pray or how you pray is any different or not." He chuckled. I felt stupid, but I really didn't know the difference.

"There's a little difference between us, but if you want to talk, I'll be more than glad to listen."

I looked over at him. He really looked like he cared about me, even if I just met him.

"I don't know anymore." I started to explain it to him. "This whole thing is confusing."

"Can you explain a little better?" he asked.

"I just...I requested to see you because I know before the day is over, I'm going to see my new therapist, and I thought to talk to another Christian or pastor would be helpful. I don't know. I feel like a pastor actually cares about me, while a therapist is getting paid to. I wanted to tell you how I felt before I told a therapist, even if you're Catholic and I'm not." I had a negative feeling about seeing my therapist. Obviously, I know now that therapists don't get paid to care. But at that moment, that was what I did feel.

"I understand. Well, how do you feel?"

"I don't know. I guess I always knew somewhere in my heart that I was unhealthy. From the moment I started making myself puke, I knew it was unhealthy. Why else would I try to hide it? Then I knew when I started to get pale and short of breath that I was hurting myself. I knew that one day all of it would catch up to me. I guess I knew that it would kill me if I didn't make a change." I got quiet for a couple of seconds. "I just didn't know it would all catch up to me so quickly. I knew it would catch up to me. There wasn't any way of lying to myself out of that. I just didn't expect things to escalate so fast and really didn't even consider it would do this much damage to me. I thought I had more time, maybe even a couple of years, to try to get it under control for myself."

"By what you've told me, I'm guessing you've come down from the eating disorder unit of the building?" he asked.

"Yes, sir," I told him. "I just accepted Christ not too long ago, and to be honest, I'm sort of lost on where to go from here. I mean, I've been told I can be forgiven and forgive. I just don't know where to begin." I started to get choked up on my words.

"Where does one even start in asking for forgiveness for the things I've done for myself and the lies I've told about it?" I asked him.

"Have you prayed for forgiveness?" he asked.

"I have, several times," I told him. "I just don't know why I still feel this way. I just don't get it," I added. I wasn't making eye contact with him while we talked. I was looking straight ahead at the altar. I looked at the brown cross that hung off the wall behind it. The flags that hung next to them. The American flag and the New Jersey State flag on one side. The church flag and Israel's flag on the other. My face was turning red. I could feel it. I hardly felt comfortable talking about this kind of stuff to a priest, let alone a therapist.

"If you prayed for forgiveness," he said, starting to talk again, "then you shouldn't feel guilty about it. God has forgiven you. What you need to ask yourself is if you've forgiven yourself."

Truth be told, I hadn't. I was holding my relationships failing as my fault, my dad hating me as my fault, and my eating disorder as my fault.

"I don't know." I buried my face into my hands. I didn't cry as much as tears tried to force their way up.

"Let me pray over you," he said. He started praying, and to be honest, I felt the same way when he did. After he prayed, he stood up and looked down at me still sitting. "You're wondering where it all starts. Start with reading the book of John. It was very nice meeting you, Larry. I'll be seeing you again soon." He turned around and walked away, and I sat there for a couple of minutes before Diane came and collected us to bring us back upstairs.

## CHAPTER 16

Bethany was already gone by the time we got back upstairs. Well, she was in her room with her parents as they were setting up her discharge papers. I went into my room when I got back and sat at the desk. My Bible was sitting on top of it, next to a little "welcome" note that the staff left for me. I sat there in silence for a couple of minutes. "It all begins with the book of John," he had told me. I hadn't read once since I got out of the hospital last. I hadn't read at all for myself until this point in my life. I smiled. *Let's change that,* I thought, and I opened it. I didn't know much about the Bible or how God worked. Truth be told, when I opened my Bible for the first time in that hospital room, it took me a while to even find out where the book of John was. I finally found it, though, and I read the first chapter of John. I felt confused reading it; I didn't fully understand what it was saying my first time trying to read it. I started to get irritated, and I even tried to read it out loud. I just couldn't comprehend what it was saying.

*Please help me understand!* I cried out to God. *Please, I want to understand. But I need help to do so.*

"What do you need help with?" someone asked. I turned and looked, and a woman was standing in my room. "I'm sorry for just coming in. You're Larry, right?" she asked.

"Yeah, I am. I'm sorry, I'm just trying to read this Bible my sister got me, and to be honest, I'm confused trying to understand what it's saying." I gave a fake chuckle.

"Where are you reading?" she asked. I told her what I was reading, and she came over to my desk and looked down at the Bible.

"I don't understand who 'the witness of the light' is,'" I said. "I was fine until I got there," I explained.

"That's John the Baptist. He came to prepare the way for the Lord," she said. "Jesus came, but first John did to prepare the way for Him. Does that make sense?"

I nodded and asked if John the Baptist wrote the book. She smiled at me.

"No." She laughed a little. "There are a couple of different Johns. There's John the Baptist, who prepared the way for Jesus, and then the disciple of Jesus whose name was John. He was the one who wrote it." I looked up at her, looking a little puzzled.

"Oh! Forgive me," she said, laughing. "I'm sorry, my name is Christina. I'm your therapist. I'm a pastor's kid, though, so I know a few things about the Bible from where I grew up with it."

I stood up and shook her hand.

"I just wanted to come in and introduce myself and maybe get our first session done now, if you'd like?" she asked. "If you're not ready yet, though, I can come back in a bit."

"No, no. We can do it now," I told her.

She went over and sat down on the couch, and I sat on my bed. She explained to me the same thing that Dr. Beech said. Everything I told her would be confidential unless I gave plans on harming myself or others. Also, if I admitted to purging or any other eating disorder symptoms, she would have to tell my team about it. She also explained to me that we would be meeting every day Monday through Friday and have the weekends off from it. Though, if I desperately needed to talk to someone, other social workers in the hospital could come up and talk to me.

    She went over basic things with me for our first session. My age, birthday, where I was from, where I went to school. The same things Dr. Beech did for the most part when I saw him. I answered all her questions.

    "Okay," she said. "Now, I am going to ask the most specific questions about you and your eating disorder." I nodded. She first started asking what symptoms I had. I told her the same things I told Dr. Smith during my intake.

    "I saw you reading the Bible, so I'm going to make a safe assumption that you're a Christian?" she asked. I nodded. "Okay, great, so my next question is, How big of a role do you want religion to play in your recovery? On a scale of 1 to 10."

    "I have to be honest. Becoming a Christian is one of the things that pushed me to want to get better. I'll say 10." I smiled at her. It's amazing how many things can change in just a short period. A month ago, I could have sworn I didn't believe in God, and now I did. A few months before that, my mom was still alive and I was at home with her. Now I must call home a hospital two hours away from where I lived.

    "How do you feel about having to be here?" Christina asked.

    I sat in silence for a couple of seconds, trying to think of an answer. The question hit me. So far, I didn't hate it here, but between having nurses watch me eat and use the bathroom, I felt uncomfortable.

    "I guess…I'm happy I am here. I'm happy that I'm given this opportunity to get better." I started to get lost for words and was quiet for a few seconds. I was fully lost for words, and she could tell.

"But...?" she asked.

"I hate that I have to be here. I know, just from being here, I was given a great opportunity I know not everyone gets. A new beginning, a chance to get healthy," I said and started shaking my head. "I just hate that I need to be given that opportunity in the first place." Christina just seemed like a good person; she clearly was doing her job well, but I felt more comfortable talking to the pastor down in the chapel, though. I felt like she was just doing something she was taught in school and the pastor was telling me what was on his heart. I'm not saying her job isn't important; she clearly cared about me, as all social workers care about their patients. It just goes back to the fact I wish I didn't have to see one.

"So if I'm hearing you correctly, you're thankful to be here. You just don't like that you have to be?" she asked.

"Absolutely," I said. "It's nothing against you either, or anyone else. It's just...I don't know how to explain it. Do any of the patients really want to be here? I mean, I doubt one person wakes up excited about having to be at a hospital."

"I fully understand how you feel," she told me. "I can't imagine someone at your age who should be excited about graduating having to be here. Is there anything else?" I just shook my head no. There more I talked about it, the more I got worked up. The more I got angry.

"I'll tell you what? Just so you can get settled in, if you want, I'll excuse you from the group activities for the rest of the day. You meet with your nutritionist tomorrow morning, so that will be a good start to your treatment program." She stood up, and I stood up with her. "Just try to get out of this room a little bit. Go to the group room and hang out with Sarah and Zach a little bit." She smiled, and I did too.

"I'll see you in a bit," I said as I was following her out of the room. I started to walk down to the group room. Sarah and Zach were both sitting in front of the TV, playing some sort of Portal game.

"New guy!" Zach yelled as I was coming in.

"How long are you planning on calling me that?" I asked and chuckled.

"Until you're not new anymore. I'll give it until tomorrow," he said.

"I overheard Diane talking to one of the nurses," Sarah said. "We're getting a new patient tomorrow. Not just any patient either. Another adolescent."

"That's not good," I said, giving a laugh.

Zach yelled at the TV briefly when his character died, and he put his controller down. He turned and faced me while Sarah shut the TV off.

"Not good for them. Pretty sad, actually. But we don't get many adolescents. This unit holds around thirty patients at a time, and only four—well, three now that Bethany went home—are younger than eighteen," Zach explained. "It's very rare we get male adolescents, so it's nice to see someone else here besides me. Sarah thinks the patient coming in tomorrow is a girl. We'll see."

"Group time!" a woman sang, coming into the room. "Oh, hello! I don't believe we've met before. You must be Larry!" she told me, and she reached out and shook my hand.

"I'm Kelly. I'm the nutritionist here on site," she said. She went to pull up a chair and sat in front of the TV with her back turned to it. I went over and sat on the couch next to Sarah. I knew I was excused from group, but the alternative to not going would be to sit in my room. So group it was.

"Now, Larry, I don't know if they explained the weekly schedule to you, but on Thursday afternoon, I teach a nutrition class," she said. I nodded. She explained Thursday's afternoon schedule better to me. For the most part, the adults and the adolescent groups were kept separate. While we had our nutrition group in our group room, the adults were having one in their group room as well. After that group, we had one more group, the last group before dinner, and it was typically a game of some sort to cool down for the day. That group was led by Matt.

For the hour, Kelly taught on the importance of nutrition and made us play food bingo. I sat in boredom, and I could even see Sarah fighting to stay awake during the class too. Zach was staring at Kelly with a blank stare that made me try my best not to laugh every time I looked at him. For my first group, it wasn't too well. I didn't know what was worse, the fact we were playing food bingo or how slow the hour seemed to drag by. When it finally ended and Kelly left the room, Sarah sighed.

"Please tell me other groups are more interesting than that," I said.

"They are," she said, letting out a yawn. "Kelly is sweet. It's just our groups are a little boring because there aren't enough people to participate. That's why we get excited when we learn another teenager is showing up."

"Geez," I said. "I didn't think I was going to make it," I said, laughing.

"Welcome to Princeton," she said, laughing with me.

"Well, I have to use the bathroom before our last group," I said, standing up. "I'll be back."

I started walking to my room and remembered halfway there that I needed a nurse to unlock my bathroom. I walked back to the nursing station to get one of them. Honestly, I didn't know what felt more awkward, having a nurse listen to me use the bathroom or having to ask them to come unlock it for me and walk back to my room with me in awkward silence because having a nurse escort me to my bathroom didn't feel like the best time to spark up a conversation with someone. *Let's get this over with,* I thought to myself. The thought of Sarah saying, "Welcome to Princeton," went through my head when I got ready to ask a nurse for the bathroom. It made me smile.

For dinner that night, I had the same thing I had at lunch, but with an ice cream cup and fruit added to it. I didn't meet with my nutritionist yet, so I didn't get to work with a meal plan yet, so I got what the hospital was specializing in that day. In front of the dining hall was a high table with a chair in it. Matt sat in it and watched us eat, for obvious reasons.

"Okay, everyone," he said. "Let's go over if we accomplished our goals and one thing were thankful and proud of." He started at the adult table and worked around. One by one everyone said whether or not they completed some goal, and one thing they were thankful and proud of themselves for.

"Larry," Matt said when it got to our table. "I know this is probably confusing for you, so let me explain. Every morning at breakfast, we make a goal for the day and I write it down. I'd prefer you say what the goal is, but if it's personal, that's fine. At dinner, we tell everyone if we accomplished the goal, and one thing we are thankful for and one thing we are proud of."

"That's fun," I told him.

"Yeah, so I know you probably didn't make a goal this morning, but if you want to say something you're thankful or proud of, you can. But if not, we won't put you on the spot," he said with a big grin on his face.

"Ugh." I thought about it for a couple of seconds. "Well, I'm thankful for God. I'm new to my faith, but I'm very thankful for it. I guess I'm just proud of myself for coming here."

"I'm proud of you too," Sarah whispered to me.

The rest of the group went. I finished my meal again, and I got extremely nervous while I was eating it. I started to feel hot and even sweated while eating. Matt, to keep people's mind off the food they were eating, usually played a game with everyone. He gave riddles to think about too. Anything to keep our mind off the fact that we are eating. It helped a lot, but all I could focus on was eating. I felt uncomfortable, too, knowing he and the nurses were watching us eat as well. If we attempted anything we weren't supposed to do, then we'd get caught. Just the feeling of having someone constantly down our back when we ate, when we used the bathroom, and even when we slept gave me a very uncomfortable feeling.

When dinner was finished, it was visitor time. I, of course, didn't have any visitors that night, so I went to lie in bed. The nurses came by with a cart and let me sign out my cell phone, so for the next few hours, I lay in my new room, scrolling through Facebook. It was too early to tell if it was going well or not, so I didn't call Brandon or Emily. Once during visitor hours, I went to the nursing station and saw Sarah in the group room with her parents; they were watching the TV. Spending time together like a family should. It made me smile. I went back to my room.

The first night was the hardest, no doubt about that. After the nurse collected my phone, I lay on my side, staring out the window. I watched the parking lot lights and the streetlights light up the night sky. Even though it was dark, I could see the lights of downtown Princeton light up the church steeple. My first night was hard to deal with. The facility and unit were better than I pictured in my mind. The worst part about the first night was knowing I was two hours away from home. Right then, Emily was probably up and was emotional while Blake did his best to try to comfort her. Brandon was probably worried about me, but no matter how hard Lilly pushed him, he wouldn't tell her how he felt about my being here. Dad? He was probably drunk and passed out in his chair. He had no idea what hospital I was in or the reason I was even there or how long I'd be there. Even if he did, would he care?

I buried my face in my pillow and tried my best to fall asleep, but I couldn't. Someone new was going to be there tomorrow. Whether they were a boy or girl, I hoped he or she was doing better than me. If they were stressed or not, I hoped they felt better than I was. I lay in bed and prayed in my heart. About an hour after that, sleep finally found me.

# CHAPTER 17

I woke up to the sound of a nurse rolling a cart into my room. The wheels squeaked as she pushed it across the tile floor. I sat up in bed and rubbed my eyes, trying to figure out what was going on.

"Good morning," she said and laid a hospital gown on my bed.

"Everything okay?" I asked in a soft voice. I still wasn't fully awake yet.

"Yes, dear. Everything is fine. I'm just coming in to get your temperature and blood pressure while you're sitting and again while you're standing." She put the cuff on me and took it while the thermometer sat in my mouth. Both dinged. "Very good. Now, can you stand up for me?" she asked. I did. According to the clock on the wall next to the window, it was 5:30 a.m. My eyes started to squint.

"Very good," she said. "Now, I want you to get changed into the hospital gown I put on your bed. Then you go down the hall to get weighed. Make sure you're wearing nothing underneath it. After that, you can either go to the group room or rest in bed."

I nodded.

"I see you're still on bathroom observations, so a nurse will come and help you take a shower shortly."

*Help me take a shower?* I thought to myself. What did that supposed to mean? Those words woke me up enough to start getting my day ready. When the nurse left with the cart, I changed out of my clothes and put the gown on. It didn't have a back to it, just string to tie the back up, so against the nurse's wish, I kept my underwear on. I doubt they'd care or even notice. The second I walked into the hallway, I could see a few people lined up to get weighed. There was a room about the size of a walk-in closet where there was a nurse with a cart, and behind the curtain was where people would stand to get weighed. I went up and saw Dean standing and talking to another girl, so I went up and talked to him.

"Good morning," I said.

"Aye, man. Another day in paradise, right?" His voice still sounded sleepy. "Have you met Michelle?" He pointed at the girl he was talking to.

"I'm Larry," I told her. I would have shaken her hand, but all of us were holding the back of our gowns closed. "Do we have to do this every morning?" I asked.

"Yeah, unfortunately. The third-shift nurses do it before first shift comes in and takes over for the day," Dean said. The nurse from the room where the scale was at called for the next person in line.

"Why don't you go?" Michelle asked. "Get your first morning done." I nodded and went in.

"Good morning," she said. "Is this your first morning?" I told her yes. "Well, hello! I'm Rebekah. I'm head of the third-shift staff." I told her my name, and she smiled. She told me to step behind the curtain and stand on the scale. As I did, she shut the door slightly so no one from the hallway could see in.

"Okay, now, no one can see. Take your gown off for me."

I did. I felt humiliated. Right in front of me, while I was standing on my scale, was a sign that said, "Don't ask the nurse for your weight!"

I couldn't use the bathroom without a nurse watching, I couldn't take a shower without a nurse watching me, and now I was finding out I had to get weighed every morning without even knowing what had changed.

"Okay," she said. "You're all set, Larry."

I put my gown back on. "It was nice meeting you," I said as I walked past her. I still felt exhausted, so I headed back to my room to get more sleep until the nurse arrive so I could shower.

"I'll see you later on!" I said to Dean as I walked past him and went back to my room and lay in bed.

I felt so tired I could hardly stand. I felt a mixture of tiredness and hunger. Just a few days ago, if I was hungry, I would roll over and lie with my stomach pressed against my fists to get rid of the hunger pangs. Now I knew I was going to have to go to breakfast. I started to doze off, and right as I was about to, a nurse came in for my shower.

The other nurse worded it wrong. She didn't help me shower; she unlocked my bathroom and sat outside the bathroom and listened as I was in there. She told me I only had fifteen minutes to shower. When I got out and got dried and put clothes on, I started brushing my teeth. When I was, she watched me brush to make sure I didn't plan on using my toothbrush for other purposes. It wasn't as bad or as awkward as I thought. When I got done, I thanked the nurse for unlocking the bathroom and crawled back into bed. I was wearing a pair of jeans and T-shirt. My sneakers were on the floor next to my bed. I started to pray in my heart and to thank God for the morning and fell back asleep.

"Breakfast time! Please come down to the dining hall!" a loud voice said over the speaker next to me, and I woke up. I looked out the window, and the sun was mostly up. The clock read 6:30 a.m. I sat up in bed feeling a lot more energized than I did an hour ago and put my shoes on and went out to meet the day. I went to grab my tray. This morning it had bacon, an egg-and-cheese omelet, cut strawberries, and a cup of coffee. Along with our meals, we all had to drink a certain amount of water.

"Good morning," Sarah said. She was walking with a tray and sat down on the chair next to mine. She and Zach were still both in their pajamas. Matter of fact, most people were, besides Dean and me.

"You are way too dressed up for the morning," Sarah said, laughing while looking at me.

"I didn't realize it was casual morning," I said, laughing. "Next time I'll wear a tux."

"Good comeback," Sarah said. "I'll give you that one. You look cute, though, dressed up normally while the rest of us are slacking. Last night, though, I told my mom we got a new adolescent here. She wanted me to say hello to you for her." I gave her smile and turned and looked at my food. I started to say grace. I prayed over my food, not just to thank God for it, but also to pray that I could eat it without getting worried. I felt stressed and anxious about eating it the second I grabbed the tray off the cart.

"Bone apple tea, guys," Zach said, opening his milk and rubbing his tired eyes. I couldn't help but laugh.

"Good morning!" Diane said a couple of minutes later. She came and sat in the same seat Matt sat in last night. "Okay, guys, let's make our goals for today." She pulled out a sheet of paper and a pen.

"Larry," she called me. "It's your first morning here. Why don't you start?" I sat and thought for a couple of seconds. I couldn't think of anything right away.

"You straight put my man on the spot," Zach said, laughing from across the table. "If you don't mind, Larry, I can go first and give you time to think." I nodded and started laughing again.

"I got to get homework done today," Zach said. "Yeah, I'll do that."

"I'll follow with him," Sarah added. "I got homework to do." The question came back to me on my goal.

"I'd like to read my Bible a little bit. I need to catch up on that," I said and looked at her. As easy as that sounded, saying my first goal felt like pulling a Band-Aid. Diane smiled and wrote down what we all said and went on the next table.

"When do we do homework?" I asked Sarah.

"About forty minutes after lunch, there's a classroom by the nursing station. We sit in there with a home instructor and do homework our school sends us. We do schoolwork from then until around the time lunch starts. After that, we're done for the day school-wise, then, as you saw yesterday, we start our groups," Sarah explained. "Whenever your therapist or psychiatrist comes and gets you to meet is up to them. When it's your turn, they'll just come and find you."

I wish I could say my breakfast that morning was a "third time's the charm" thing, but it wasn't. I felt anxiety eating that morning, just like I did the last two meals. I started to get hot and could feel sweat starting to roll down my forehead as I ate. I was to the point of tearing up. *I can't do this,* I thought to myself. *I really can't do this.* I was starting to feel lost in my thoughts after finishing my omelet and coffee. Finally, someone called my name.

"Larry!" I looked up. Dr. Smith was standing outside the dining hall in the hallway. I overheard him tell Diane to have my bacon and fruit wrapped up. I could eat it as one of my snacks later. He walked up closer to me and said in a softer voice so only my table could hear him, "Let's have our daily meeting now. C'mon."

I stood up and followed him down to my hall in silence.

"You know, we normally aren't allowed to do that," Dr. Smith said as he turned my bedroom light on. He walked in, and I followed behind him. I took a seat on my bed, and he sat on the couch that was next to my nightstand. "I could tell just by watching you, though, you looked like you were getting ready to go into a panic attack." I sat in silence; I didn't know how to reply.

"Have you've been getting those lately?" he asked.

I managed to make myself talk. "I normally feel the way I do after a binge episode. I normally feel somewhat better after I purge, though," I said. "They've gotten worse since I started eating here. They seem to be getting worse every meal."

"Have you ever been on medication to treat anxiety?" he asked.

"No," I said. "No, I've never been on medication before."

"I'd like to try that," he said. "To see how it works. What I'm going to do is, I'm going to prescribe something called Vistaril. It's an anxiety medication."

I looked at him and didn't say anything again.

"I just want you to try it a little to see how it works for you," he said. "If it doesn't work or you don't like it, we can try something else." He smiled at me.

"Thank you, Doc," I said.

He stood up. "Kelly, your nutritionist, she should be here in a couple of minutes. If you want to wait in your room for now, I'll send her to come get you. You need to start making your meal plan so you can pick what you want to eat for lunch. It'll give you some freedom."

I lay back in bed and sat. Kelly came in a few moments later.

Kelly explained to me how meals worked. The meal plans started off in colors. Since it was my first day here, I was on the "white" plan. As I progressed through the program, though, and moved up in meal plans, the amount of food that I ate would increase, and so would the amount of water I had to drink.

"Every day, you must eat a certain amount of vegetables, fruit, dairy, starch, meat or meat supplement, and a supplement. As you move up in your meal plan, the amount of each food group you must eat will go up."

I sat in bed, trying my best not to get upset with her talking about this.

"Do you have any food allergies?"

I said no.

"Do you have a certain meal plan you want to follow? Like, are you a vegetarian, or do you have a religious dietary plan you need to follow?"

I said no to that question as well.

"Very good," she said, and she handed me a couple sheets of paper and a menu of all the food I could choose from. Each sheet of paper had fill-in-the-blanks I had to fill on what I wanted to eat for my meal that day.

"Now, all you have to do is fill those in and bring them to my office when you're down. If I'm not there when you're down, just slide them under my door," she said.

"Thank you," I forced myself to say as she walked out of the room.

I knew the amount of food I was eating for the past few meals was light, but I didn't realize they increased. I thought it was hard enough to eat what I already had, let alone getting bigger portions. I sat in my room for a couple of moments, looking over the menus and what I could choose from. Right then, with the meal plan I was on, I only had to choose a few things and I was done. It wasn't even lunchtime yet, and I was already feeling stressed out from how breakfast went, and now having to make a meal plan on top of that made me even more anxious. I continued to look through my meal plans until Sarah knocked on my door to tell me it was time for us to go to our class.

The home instructor's name was Brandy. She was a middle-aged blond woman. She was very pretty, and she wore glasses. The second I got into the class, she introduced herself like everyone else did. I had my menus with me, and I was going to work on them when I got done with whatever work my school sent in for me to do.

"I only have one rule when it comes to the class," she said. "I don't mind what you do after your work is finished, but I don't want you to work on your menus or talk about food."

I hurried up and slid my menus into a binder that was sitting on the table and sat down next to Sarah, who was trying her best not to laugh at me. Zach sat down across the table, working on algebra homework.

"Now, I called your school, and apparently, they never told your teachers that you were being put into the inpatient program. So for today, I don't have any work for you to do. So if you want, you can either read, draw, or do whatever you need to drag the time out. There's a shelf of books over on the shelf." I turned and look, and one of the first books I saw was a Bible. I left mine in my room, so I went over and grabbed it off the shelf and sat back down next to Sarah. I was halfway through John, so I opened back up and started reading.

"You should be a preacher," Zach said.

"I haven't been a believer that long," I said. "I'm not sure if that's something I'd be cut out for."

"I'm not the most religious person alive, but I believe God is real. I doubt anything would be out of the realm of possibility with Him. If you're not cut for it, He can make you."

I smiled. I never thought of it that way. I doubt Zach even meant anything serious when he said that, but that was something I really needed to hear.

We sat in silence for the most part. Sarah was working on some history essay, while Zach was working on math. It was hard to do big projects for school here because it would be hard to get the work back to the teachers at our school. Most of the people who came to this program were hours away from home. I was over two hours away from home, so we could only do work that could be faxed back to the school, nothing too big.

I sat reading until there was a knock on the door. Christina popped her head in the room.

"Larry," she said.

I looked up, expecting her to say something.

"It's your turn for your therapy session," Sarah said.

"Oh!" I said and got up quickly to go meet Christina at the door. She took me, and we walked down to my room. On the way down, we were making small talk, how we were. I asked her what she had planned for the weekend because it was Friday. When we got to my room, I went to sit on my bed again and Christina pulled up a chair from the desk and sat across from me.

"Our meeting ended somewhat early yesterday," Christina said. "There are few more things I'd like to go over with you."

"Where would you like to start?" I asked.

"Well, I'd like to get a picture of what your homelife is like," she said. "I wasn't there when you got admitted here and did your intake, but Diane and Dr. Smith brought it to my attention that it was your sister and your brother who brought you in?"

"My sister, yes," I said. "Brandon, though, the other guy, as close as we are, he isn't my brother. Though I will say he's the closest thing I have to a brother."

"Any more siblings?" she asked.

"No," I said. "My sister is my only sibling. I live with her and her husband, Blake."

"Where are you parents?" she asked.

I was quiet for a couple of seconds. I knew I would have to talk about them; I also knew that doing so would be extremely difficult for me to do. I'd gotten into the habit of looking down at my hands when I got put into an uncomfortable situation.

"Larry?" Christina asked.

"My mom died at the beginning of the school year," I said. "I was at school, and she got into a car accident. She unfortunately didn't recover from it, and I believe she died at the scene."

"I'm so sorry," Christina said. "That must have been hard on both you and your sister."

"My dad and I don't get along. He drinks a lot, and I don't like being around it. So I moved in with my sister," I told her. I knew I would have to tell her about what really happened. I wanted to try to beat around the bush as much as I could, though.

"How'd that happen?" she asked. "Or what made you move out?"

"He made it clear he didn't want me there," I told her. "The night my mom died, we got into a huge argument. He said he didn't love me and told me I could get out for all he cared, so I did."

"Were you already dealing with an eating disorder?" she asked me.

"No," I explained. "I think everything that happened was one of the things that triggered it, though." I was to the point of tears, and I was trying my best to hold them in. Christina knew what I was doing. She was even getting upset by the things I was telling her.

"You don't have to hold it in anymore, Larry. Please let it out. That's why you're here."

I started crying, and she got tissues out of her bag and handed them to me. As I was wiping my face, she put her hand on my shoulder.

"Do you feel like it's a control thing? A lot of people with eating disorders feel like their weight is the only thing they can control. That's one of the reasons they hang on to it," she told me.

"Yeah," I said. "To be honest, that's exactly how I feel." Christina sat back down and looked at her notes. She started to look puzzled.

"I wonder why your dad would say those things to you," she said.

"I was unplanned," I said.

She looked even more confused.

"Most of us are unplanned. That can't be the only reason," she said. "I don't think he hates you. What I want you to know is, when someone gets an addiction—you mentioned he drinks a lot—they lose who they really are."

I nodded.

"Larry, this has nothing to do with you," she said. "Your dad is just dealing with his own problems, and he's taking it out on you. You didn't do anything wrong."

I started to tear up again. She smiled and patted me on the shoulder again.

For the rest of the time, we continued to talk about my family and my friends. I told her about Brandon and the stuff we pulled while at school, and I told her more about choir and how we'd hang out in the choir room before we'd go to work. It made me realize even more that when everything happened, Brandon was always a friend that I could depend on. He even missed school to drive up with me and my sister so I could do my intake. Afterward, we went into deeper details on my living situation. How long I lived with my sister, what my living situation was like with her, how Blake was. Everything. By the time the hour was up, I started to feel better than when the appointment first started today.

"Well, Larry, that's about all the time I have for us today. So we can get ready to wrap things up, and lunch is going to start in a couple of minutes," she said.

"Great," I said. I was already starting to get anxious again.

"I would like to set up a family therapy session," she said. "With you, your sister, and Blake."

"That's fine," I said. As I said that, someone spoke over the speaker that it was lunchtime and we should begin to head down.

"I'll work out more details on that," she said. "Enjoy lunch." She walked out of my room, and I followed.

I had started walking down the hall on my way to the dining hall when Sarah walked over to me.

"The new person is here!" she said. "It's a girl. I don't think she'll be at lunch, but she should be in group after lunch, though."

"Well, that's nice, I guess," I said.

"Good that we have another teenager here. But bad for the reason that she's here," she said. "She seems nice. I didn't talk to her much, but I think she said her name is Lucy."

*Lucy, huh?* I thought to myself. *That's a pretty name.*

I didn't turn in my menus yet, so for lunch I had a hot dog, mac and cheese, chopped carrots, and a ginger ale. I sat messing with my mac and cheese with my fork, staring at my plate. Slowly picking and eating at what was there.

"I think the new girl is around our age," Sarah said. She looked a little upset.

"Are you okay?" I asked.

Sarah looked at her plate and back at me. "They upped my meal plan. I just…I feel uncomfortable is all," she said. Matt interrupted and told us to not discuss meal plans at the table. Sarah looked at me and shrugged her shoulders.

"You got this," I whispered to her. "Everything will be okay." Hoping to make her feel better, I took a bite out of my food. She smiled as I took a bite and made a weird face at her.

"Smack the pony and leave," Zach said. Sarah laughed, almost choking on the water she was drinking.

"What's funny?" I asked.

"We're coming up with funny ways to say food again. I'm calling your Mac and Cheese, smack the pony and leave." He laughed as I was saying it, which made Sarah laugh even more. Sarah started to smile as she took more bites out of her food, and she looked at the both of us.

This was only my second day at the unit. I knew I hadn't been here that long, but I was already starting to feel a strong friendship starting to build with Zach and Sarah, especially Sarah. It made me upset to see her uncomfortable; I wish I could do more to help her, but it also made me think that this might be how Emily felt when I was taking care of myself. For the rest of lunchtime, we sat and joked around about different ways of pronouncing food and trying to come up with different ways to say them. The more we joked around and laughed, the more Sarah smiled, and she ended up completing her meal. So did Zach and I. I think it's fair to say I had started to get used to being here. I was starting to make the best of it.

## CHAPTER 18

"Hey, Larry!" Dean yelled to me as I was walking back to the group room. Lunch was over, and we had a half-hour before our next group started, so I used the bathroom and was heading back.

"Hey, bro," I said.

"I was just coming up to check to see how you were handling everything here so far. You've been here for a day so far."

"I'm doing okay." I smiled. "I think I'm finally accepting that I'm here. I still don't like it, but I'm getting used to it."

"Good, man!" he said. "I'm heading back to my room to take a short nap. Catch up with me later, though, bro." He walked off the other direction, while I kept walking toward to group room.

I walked in and saw Zach sitting close to the TV, again playing Minecraft. Sarah was sitting at the table, working on her menus, and the new girl was sitting on the couch. She was beautiful.

"Hey, Larry!" Sarah called out to me. "That's Lucy."

I looked back at her, and she smiled and held her hand up and gave a short wave. I went over and sat down on the opposite side of the couch as her. Again, she was beautiful. She had long blond hair and green eyes. She was wearing blue jeans and a short-sleeve button-up. She had black gloves on though. Overall, though, I couldn't help but notice that she was one of the most beautiful girls I'd ever seen.

"Hello," I said as I was sitting down.

"Hi," she said in a soft voice, almost like a whisper. I could tell she was uncomfortable being here, that she didn't want to be here. I couldn't blame her; I felt just like she did just twenty-four hours ago.

"Are you okay?" I asked. She just nodded. She didn't want to talk much yet, and again, I fully understood if she didn't.

"Hey, Larry," Zach called out. His eyes were still focused on the TV while he played his video game. "Congrats, bro. You're no longer the new guy. But we can't call Lucy the new guy, for obvious reasons. So you're still technically the new guy."

"Zach, be quiet and play your video game," Sarah said.

"Okay," he uttered back. Lucy smiled at that; her smile was as beautiful as she was. Sarah finished her menus and put them into her binder, then came over to the couch.

"Hey, can you move over? If you don't mind, I like sitting with the armrest," Sarah said.

I moved over, and Sarah sat down. I was between Sarah and Lucy. Sarah tried talking to Lucy, too, but she didn't talk much. Even if she did, they were only one-word answers. She accomplished getting her to talk more than I did, though. Diane came into the room.

For our next group, on Friday's after lunch, the adolescents had group therapy. Diane came in and pulled up a chair and told Zach to turn the game off and come sit with the rest of us. He sat on the recliner next to the couch.

"Okay, guys," Diane said, "since we have a new person joining us today, as an icebreaker, let's all go around the room and say our name and our favorite TV shows." She started. Surprisingly, Sarah, Zach, and I said *The Office*. When it came to Lucy, she quietly said her name and said *Supernatural*. Diane started by asking everyone how they were doing and what was new with our treatment process.

"Well, I have good news," Zach said. "I just got told today by Dr. Smith that this would be my last week. They plan on sending me home a week from today." Diane congratulated him. I reached over and patted him on the back.

"Are there any challenges you are worried about facing?" Diane asked. "About leaving?" Zach shook his head no and explained that he was just happy to be going home; he'd been there a while, so he was happy about going home and seeing his family. I was happy but wished I could go home too.

"How about you, Larry?" Diane asked. "How have you been since you've been here?"

I took a couple of seconds to think of an answer to give her.

"Well, to be honest, not much has happened. Though I'm happy for Zach, I'm going to be sad to see him leave." I looked over at him and smiled and looked back at her. "Christina wants to set up a family therapy session with my sister and her husband."

"Not your parents?" she asked.

I saved most of the details, but I explained what happened to my mother and that my dad threw me out. I explained I lived with my sister because of it. Sarah looked shocked that something like that happened.

"I'm really sorry that you got put into that position. I can't imagine how that would affect someone your age. How have you been handling that?" Diane asked.

"At first, not too well. But I'm here, and my faith in Jesus has been a big help so far. I've been reading the Bible, and it's been bringing me joy." Diane smiled.

Sarah went next and talked about how this experience had brought her and her parents closer together. Sarah had only been here for a week, but she felt that she could have a better relationship with her parents now that she was not hiding anything from them.

When it was Lucy's turn to speak, she didn't say anything. Diane even tried to get her to speak in a group. She didn't want to say anything to her either. Diane even tried asking her simple questions, like if the drive here was easy for her, but she didn't want to talk about that either. Diane gave up on trying to speak to her, and I knew Lucy was sad, and it made me upset that she was so distraught about being here that she couldn't even talk in group. Zach started sharing about his feeling about leaving next week. Diane put her attention on him.

I turned my head and looked at Lucy.

"Hey," I whispered to her. She looked at me. "It's going to be okay. If you ever need anything, I'm here. It might be easier to talk to another patient than to staff at first." I remember Dean telling me that yesterday at lunch, so I extended the same invitation to her. She smiled at me, which made me smile too.

The rest of the day went by smoothly. They didn't have any groups after that on Friday; the only rule was, we couldn't stay in our rooms. We had to be in the group room with one another in the replacement of the group. I sat on the couch, reading my Bible, as Zach and Sarah watched a show on Netflix. Lucy was on the couch across from me, looking at the TV, but she was still being quiet. After an episode, Sarah pulled out the game Sorry and set it up for us to play. Lucy joined us and still didn't say much. I guessed she just had a lot on her mind. If she left something at home or missed something at home, all that on top of being here wasn't the easiest thing to deal with.

When dinner rolled around, it didn't get any better.

"Okay, guys," Matt said, sitting up in his chair. "Let's go over our goals today." Normal routine. Everyone went over if they completed their goal and what they were proud of and thankful for. I was sitting in the same spot I normally sat in. Sarah and Zach did too. Lucy grabbed her tray and sat across the table from us—her dark-green eyes were mesmerizing.

"Let's start with the teenage table," Matt said.

Both Zach and Sarah completed their goal. I added that I completed mine too.

"I'm proud of myself for making through my first full day, and I'm thankful for making friends here," I said. Matt explained the goal of the day to Lucy and asked her if she wanted to say what she was proud of and thankful for. She continued on being quiet and didn't add anything.

It took praying and a lot of silent panicking, but I managed to complete my meal. By the time dinner was finished, though, and we could leave the table, Lucy wasn't even a quarter of the way done. I wanted to stay and wait for her in case she needed someone, but Matt told me I couldn't stay at the table if I was finished eating. So I went back to my room.

A nurse came by a few moments later, and I signed out my cell phone. I answered a few texts sent by Brandon and Emily. Emily was at work, but Brandon called me as soon as I texted him back.

"Big man!" I said as I answered the phone.

"Hey, brother man, how are things going? How is it?" he said. I heard Lilly in the background yell, "Hi, Larry!"

"Hey, guys!" I yelled into the phone. "Things are doing good right now! I'm making friends and getting through this."

"Great, man! I'm so proud of you," he said. "Hey, Lilly and I are about to go into the movies, so we can't call now, but keep me posted. Give me a call in a few hours if you still have your phone on you."

"Will do, bro," I told him. He said bye, and I did too. A movie didn't sound like a bad idea. It would be better if I got out of my room, too, instead of scrolling through Facebook or texting. I put my phone on my bed and left my room to see if Sarah or Zach were in the group room. It was a Friday night, and we could stay up an extra hour later than normal because of the weekend. Maybe they would want to watch a movie on Netflix. If they didn't have any visitors, that is.

When I got to the group room, I stood across the hall from it by the nursing station. The door was shut. Lucy was sitting on the couch, and a woman was in there with her with who appeared to be her mother. Her mom was yelling at her. I could hear it through the shut door.

"I shouldn't have to get a call from the doctor here saying you didn't complete your meal!" the woman yelled at her. Lucy said something back, but I couldn't hear her. I could hardly hear her mom yelling at her.

"I don't care what you think or if you don't want to be here!" the woman kept yelling at Lucy. "You're here for a reason! You better get it together!"

*Where is the staff?* I thought to myself. I didn't want to go in and say anything, but this couldn't be helpful at all for Lucy. The woman continued yelling at her. I could see Lucy begin to cry as tears rolled down her face. She wiped them away. "I don't care how many things you miss out on. You are not leaving here! Do you understand?" she yelled.

Matt finally stepped in when he saw what was happening.

"Ma'am, if you're going to yell like that, you'd have to leave," he said.

"I'm talking to my daughter," the woman snapped back at him. So she was her mom, I realized.

"I don't care!" Matt snapped at her. "You're clearing making her upset and possibly hurting her recovery. Please leave."

"Fine!" the woman said. She snatched up her purse and jacket from the chair. "Get your act straight!" she told Lucy and pointed at her on her way out. She slammed the group room door shut behind, and Matt followed her to make sure she left.

Lucy sat on the couch, wiping tears from her eyes. I went over the nursing station and grabbed a few tissues and brought them into the group room. I walked up and handed them to her and sat on the couch next to her.

"I'm sorry that happened," I said.

She wiped the tears from her eyes with the tissues and didn't say a word.

"Do you want to talk about it?" I asked her.

She shook her head no.

I sat for a couple more seconds before I spoke again. "You know, the biggest obstacle I'm facing while being here is being far away from home. I'm a little over two hours away. I miss my friends and sister." I threw in a fake chuckle. "I really miss my own bed, to be honest. Nothing against the hospital ones, but I feel a little too tall for them."

Lucy stopped wiping her tears and just looked at me while I talked.

"How far away are you from home?" I asked.

"Pretty far," she said. She didn't give a number, but at least she was saying something to me. I smiled at her. I couldn't get over her beauty. She pulled the hair off her face and put it behind her ears.

"I know you don't want to talk about whatever just happened, but I know talking to someone can help, even if it's not about what's bothering you. It can be about anything." I stood up. "I'm in 510. If you ever do need to talk, just come find me," I said and started to walk toward the door.

Right as I got to the door, she called my name. I turned around and looked at her. She was hesitant, but she finally talked.

"I'm an hour and a half away from home," she said. "Please stay if you'd like."

I turned around and sat down on the recliner next to the couch. "I'm more than happy to," I told her.

"I'm sorry for being quiet all day. It's been a stressful day, and as you can see from my mother, she wasn't making it any better for me. She's been acting like this whole thing is on her. I've just been stressed out is all." Her voice was still soft and quiet. When she talked, it sounded almost like a whisper. She changed into different clothes, and now she was wearing black sweatpants and a Pittsburg Penguins T-shirt.

"I live with my dad. My mom and he are divorced, and she's too busy, so I live with him. Ever since I moved in with him, though, she's just been rude and abusive toward me about it ever since." She looked at me and shook her head. "I'm sorry for rambling," she said.

"No, don't apologize!" I said. "I understand. My dad has a drinking problem, and I had to move in with my sister because of it. He got really bad when my mom passed."

"How long did you stay with your dad after your mom passed?" she asked me.

I wanted to avoid that question. I hesitated on answering it, but I did.

"He kicked me out the same day my mom died," I said with shame.

Her eyes got big, and she looked shocked. "That's terrible!" she said. "I'm so sorry that happened to you."

I shook my head and brushed it off like it was nothing. I hated to admit it, but I was used to my dad not being around. It upset me, and I didn't think it was something that anyone should have to get used to, but my dad not being around was a new normal for me.

Lucy and I sat in the group room and talked for over an hour, just about home and school. I told her about my friends, and she told me about her. I even told her part of the story on how I ended up here. I told her a few jokes, and she laughed. One of the most beautiful things I ever had seen was her smiling and laughing. When I saw her laugh that first night of meeting her, my heart skipped a beat. When we talked that night, I felt so happy that I forgot we were even in a hospital. She didn't talk until that night, but she made up for it. Everything about the hospital that made me uncomfortable and made me wish I weren't there, it all faded away talking to her.

"Can I ask you something?" she asked.

"Absolutely," I said. "What is it?"

"Earlier today, you were reading the Bible before group. During group, you also made mention that you've been holding it together well because of your faith. I've been trying my best to hold on to faith, but I just can't see God in all this. Like you, you seem nice. You didn't deserve what happened to your parents. Why would God allow something like that? How do we hold faith when things like this happen?"

I shook my head. I didn't know what to say to that. It was a good question, but I couldn't think of an answer.

"I'm not sure. I'm really new to the faith. I haven't even been a Christian a full month yet. But what I do know is this: Jesus loves me, and He also loves you. Now, I don't think being a Christian will help us avoid all bad things in our lives. But it certainly is nice to have God to run to when bad things do happen," I told her.

She looked at me, and her face lit up with joy.

"I know there are probably better answers to that out there," she told me, "but right here, at this moment in time, that's exactly what I needed to hear. You should be a preacher."

*Wow, the second person that's told me today,* I thought to myself. I had never thought about being a pastor before today. I knew I didn't know as much about the Bible as I should to be one. I was new to the faith too. Right then, though, maybe it was something I should consider looking into. *For now, I should continue reading the Bible and getting more familiar with the scriptures,* I figured.

"I know I need to be here," she said. "I haven't been taking care of myself the way I should, and I know I need to make a change. I'm just losing so much by being here."

"How so?" I asked.

She looked outside toward the window. The lights of downtown Princeton lit the night sky up.

"My school won't let me walk in graduation this year if I didn't come here. They said I'd be too much of a liability if I did. On top of that, I won't be able to go on my senior trip because I'll be here. I'm not allowed to go to prom either."

I started thinking after hearing that. It was so sad she couldn't go. I hadn't even thought about my senior trip, if I'd be allowed to go or if it was happening while I was in here. I hadn't thought of my prom either. When it was, if the school would let me go, or if I'd miss too many days from school to be here to be able to go.

"I'm sorry to hear that," I said. My mind went back to what I heard in the hospital. If I didn't get help or go to treatment, there would have been a chance that I wouldn't even make it to see graduation.

"It might not mean much, but at least I'm getting better. It might cost a few things, but my health is worth it. I just wish it didn't cost me to lose so many things," she added.

"I'm glad you're getting better," I said. "It might seem bad now, but in the long run, it would be worth it, and even though I wish it could have been under better circumstances, I'm glad I met you."

She began to smile and blush, then she turned her head a little before looking at me again.

"I'm glad I met you too," she said.

Around that time, a nurse came in and flickered the lights a couple of times. I was so focused on Lucy I wouldn't have noticed the nurse if she didn't flicker them.

"It's almost 11:00 p.m.," the nurse said. "I'd hate to break y'all up, but it's time to wrap up your conversation and head to bed."

"Sure thing," I told the nurse, and I looked back at Lucy. "Well, you have a good night. I'll see you tomorrow." I stood up, and as I started to walk away, she grabbed my wrist. I turned around and looked at her. She was still sitting down.

"Thank you for talking to me," she said. "I know I was being stubborn today, but after what happened earlier, it means a lot that you didn't just leave me alone."

"Of course," I said. "As long as we are in here, I'll be here for you to talk to." She stood up and gave me a quick hug before the nurses could see us.

"Good night," she said, and she walked out of the room. I couldn't help but feel myself smile. I walked out of the group room too, shutting the light off behind me. I went back to my room.

I walked slowly to my room. I didn't want the night to end, but I was excited about tomorrow. From what I got from talking to Lucy, she was a couple of months younger than me. She'd graduate the same year as me too. She went to church with her dad, but she was having a hard time believing sometimes. She wanted to go into the social work field when she graduated. She loved movies, fishing, the beach. Overall, she was an amazing person to talk to when she finally opened up and talked to me. My heart was bouncing with joy. *It's too early to catch feelings,* I kept telling myself. I needed to take my time and get to know her. Plus, we were both in an eating disorder treatment program; maybe it was not the best place to start dating someone. A million thoughts raced through my mind when I finally lay in bed. I looked up at the ceiling when I crawled in bed, and I thanked God for the night. I knew out of everyone in this hospital, no matter what unit, no matter if it was staff, patient, or visitor, I knew I was the happiest person in the hospital that night.

# CHAPTER 19

I woke up in the middle of the night. My heart was racing what felt like a million beats per minute. My fast heart rate was what woke me up. "Ahhhhh!" I yelled, throwing my hand over my chest. A heart attack? No, it couldn't be. There was no pain, and I wasn't sweating, just a fast heartbeat. I didn't know. I didn't know much about heart attacks to say if it was. Something was going on, though, and it wasn't good. I threw my hand up and pressed the button on the wall to have the nurse rush down and get me. A moment later, a nurse barged through the door.

"What's going on, Larry?" she asked.

"My chest," I said, breathing heavily. "It's beating too fast." A nurse hurried and called the cardiology unit and had a doctor rush down to look me.

"Stay calm, Larry," the nurse said. "It's going to be okay."

I moved up and sat up in bed. The nurse asked me to start taking deep breaths, breathing out through my mouth. I was doing so by the time someone from the cardiology unit got there. My heartbeat seemed to go back to normal.

*It's okay, it's okay, it's okay,* I told myself. I kept breathing heavily.

The cardiologist came in. "Is everything okay?" he asked.

"My heart," I said, pointing at my chest. "It started beating really fast. It woke me up." The doctor came over and listened to my heartbeat. He started listening to me breathe.

"Are you on any medications?" he asked.

"No, sir," I said. "Not yet, anyway. I start taking Vistaril in the morning."

He nodded and asked if I had any more symptoms. I told him no.

"I'm going to have you wear a heart monitor for the weekend," he said. "Eating disorders can take a toll on the heart. I want to see you're okay," he added, then walked out of the room. I looked at the clock, and it said it was a little past 2:00 a.m. I leaned back in my bead and sighed. A heart problem wasn't something I needed right then. Not after everything else. It took a while for the doctor to get back, and I almost fell asleep waiting for him. He finally came back right as I was about to doze off again. He put a gel on my chest and stuck a pad to it, and the heart monitor was small, about the size of a square. It clipped right on to my chest.

"I'm going to have you wear this until Monday morning," he said. "Monday morning, the head cardiologist and whoever your doctor here is will go over what it picks up, all right?"

I nodded.

"I'm sorry this woke you up," he said, chuckling, and he walked out of the office.

I lay back in my bed again. My heart was beating a little faster than normal, but that was because of how scared this just made me. I shook my head and rolled over on my side and looked at the clock. I knew I was hurting myself with bulimia, but I didn't know the extent of it. My heart finally started to slow down to what I assumed was normal, and I finally started to calm down. As the night dragged on, I finally calmed down enough to fall asleep.

# CHAPTER 20

The weekend flew by like a breeze. I didn't tell Sarah, Zach, or Lucy about my heart monitor over the weekend. Zach got something called a pass from what they told me, which was if you started doing good and kept completing your meals, they'd let you go out on a pass for the day. You'd get to leave the unit for the day; however, when you got back, though, they'd question you up and down about what you did and if you did anything eating disorder related.

I spent most of the weekend with Lucy. We watched movies on Netflix in the break room, and we played games in the group room with Sarah. I tried my best to not catch feelings for her, but the more time I spent with her, the more I started to like being around her. Between her beauty, her smile, and on top of that, her just being fun to be around in general once she opened up to me, no one in their right mind wouldn't.

I sat in my room with Dr. Smith, waiting for the cardiologist to come into the room. I filled him in on what happened over the weekend. I told him how the heartbeat woke me up but that I didn't have an episode like that for the rest of the weekend. I sat on my bed, and he sat on the couch like he normally did.

"I wish I could say things like this don't happen, but they do," Dr. Smith said. Eating disorders, they really hurt your heart. They can affect every organ in your body. It's a good thing you're here now. God knows what would have happened if you continued in your eating disorder." He looked concerned for me. I couldn't tell if he was more worried about what the cardiologist would say, or if he was happy that I was here when it happened. Seeing him concerned, though, made me even more nervous.

I started taking my anxiety medication Saturday morning like he wanted me to. It made me tired over the weekend, but overall, I felt a little better at mealtimes. I didn't feel as stressed as I normally did.

"You're young. Someone as young as you shouldn't have heart problems," he said. "No one as young as you should." My mind started to race. What if he already knew what was going on? He'd been in this field a while now; I couldn't be the first person this had happened to. Maybe he already knew from the experience? I tried to remain calm. Finally, the cardiologist came in.

"Mr. Larry," he said, walking in, "I'm Dr. Frank." He came over and shook Dr. Smith's hand, then reached over and shook mine.

"He gave us a bit of a scare over the weekend, didn't he?" Dr. Smith asked and gave a smile.

"Yes, sir," the cardiologist agreed. "Larry, after looking over what the heart monitor showed us, it looks like you have an arrhythmia."

I looked at him a little confused. I didn't know what he meant.

"You have an irregular heartbeat," he said. "The problem with eating disorders and the heart is, when you're not getting the right amount of nutrients in your body, your body starts eating at your muscle. This includes your heart. Now, when the body starts using tissues from the heart for fuel, it leaves the heart with two problems. The first problem is, it leaves the heart with less fuel to use to pump. The second problem is, the heart has fewer cells to pump with. Does that make sense?"

"Sure," I said.

"When things like this happen, a lot of things can happen with your heart. Everything from an irregular heartbeat to even cardiac arrest. The heart monitor is showing us an irregular heartbeat, one of the most common things I've seen in people who've dealt with eating disorders."

I stayed quiet. I couldn't believe I'd done something like this to myself. I felt ashamed and embarrassed.

"I'm going to prescribe you a medication I want you to take every morning after breakfast. It's called verapamil. It's a medication used to treat irregular heartbeats. We'll get you all squared away," he said.

"Thank you, Doc," I told him. He stood up, shook my hand and Dr. Smith's again, and walked out. Dr. Smith followed him to the door. Before Dr. Smith walked out of the room, he turned around and looked at me.

"Larry," he said. I turned my head and looked at him. "It's going to be okay, you know. Recovery is a hard road to go on, and I know you're disappointed with this news, but you're here for a reason, and I'm proud of you." I smiled at him, and he walked out of the room. I turned and got out of my bed too. I knew there was going to be class in about forty minutes, so maybe I could catch up with Lucy or Sarah beforehand.

The class was going by quickly. The school hadn't sent in any work for me to do, so I sat and read while Sarah worked on her homework and Zach did his algebra. Lucy was sitting next to me, working on some drawing she had to do for her art class. I was into the book of Romans in the Bible.

"You're really good," I whispered to her.

"Thank you," she whispered back and smiled and turned back to her drawing.

Just then, Dr. Smith poked his head into the room.

"Zach," he said into the room. "Our turn to meet."

Zach stood up and speed-walked out to meet Dr. Smith. With him saying he was leaving soon, he'd been more excited than ever to get out.

I wanted to give Lucy a compliment. I didn't know what to tell her, what would be too strong, what would be the plan.

"You look nice today," I whispered to her. She smiled back.

Over the weekend, she'd opened up to me more and more. We went from her being fully quiet the entire day to talking, and now we were becoming friends. I didn't just like her company; I liked her.

"Thank you," she said, smiling. "You look pretty nice today yourself." She started to look through her box of art supplies for something, then I went back to reading.

"Hey, Mrs. Brandy, I forgot some of my supplies in my room. Do you mind if I go get them?" she asked.

Brandy nodded, and she got up and left. Now it was just me and Sarah. I continued reading through my book for a couple more seconds before something bounced off my forehead and landed in front of me. It was a paper ball. I looked up, and Sarah was staring at me.

"If you don't ask her out, I will," Sarah said in a whisper jokingly.

"What are you talking about?" I said back, laughing.

"You and Lucy," she said. "Larry, I'm not dumb. I see the way you look at her when she's around. You look like a lost kid the first time he goes into an arcade. To be honest, it's kind of cute."

"I'm sorry. Why does the kid in this metaphor need to be lost in the arcade for his first time?" I answered back with a sarcastic smirk on my face.

"You know what I mean," Sarah said. "I can tell you like her. To be honest, I think she likes you too. She talks to you more than she does the rest of us. She even talks to you more than with the staff here."

"You think she likes me?" I asked. I was surprised to hear Sarah say that. I was always bad at reading people. Just look at my dad. I knew him and I didn't get along, but I never would have thought in a million years he would hate me enough to throw me out. Both my exes left me, and I never even saw any of it coming. Especially Anna. One moment we were fine, at least from what I thought, and the next moment she left me and told me I was unlovable for being unhealthy. Those words still played through my mind, not because I was still hung up on her, but because I kept thinking that maybe she was right. If she couldn't still love me for being unhealthy, if my dad couldn't love me at all, why would anyone else? I started to think thoughts like that were silly. Emily loved me, Brandon did, and I knew God did.

"I think she does. I'm not saying you should rush into things, though, but she's a pretty girl, and I can tell you enjoy being around her. So what I am saying is, play it cool and see where it goes," Sarah told me.

"I can do that," I said. "I'll do that."

"Attaboy. Keep that energy," she said. Around that time, Lucy walked back into the room.

At that moment, I saw things completely different. If she did like me, maybe I wouldn't have to try so hard to impress her. I felt more relaxed, more confident. Even though I was in treatment, I felt like I was in the best place I could be now. I should start things slow, though. I should ask for her number. I started overthinking things again. *It's not too hard. You can do this,* I kept thinking to myself. I wasn't so much as nervous about asking her for her number; I was nervous about things ending as they did in my past relationship. It took me a couple of minutes, but right as I worked up the nerve to say something to her, Zach walked in before I could say anything to her. The door closed loudly behind him, and he sat down in the table in the chair across from us. He looked down at his papers and continued working. I could tell by the way he walked in and the way he looked that he was upset.

"Zach?" Sarah asked him. "Are you all right?" He shook his head no. He didn't even look up at us.

"What's going on?" she asked him. Zach didn't say a word to her. "Zach," she said his name again.

"I'm not getting out this week," he blurted out. There was anger in his voice as he continued to rush through his schoolwork. "My weight apparently dropped, and they think I need to make more progress, so they said they're keeping me here for another week on top of this one."

Sarah didn't say anything at first; she tried to think of something to tell him, but we were all lost for words at first.

"I'm sorry," Sarah said, trying to show empathy. "But it's not too bad. We can keep pushing and you'll be out of here before you know it."

"That's bullcrap!" he snapped. "I should be getting out of here this week!"

"Zach, try to calm down!" Brandy said from her computer across the room.

Zach stood up and slammed his hands on the table and slapped his books and papers off them, and they flew into the wall.

"Don't you dare tell me to calm down! You go home every night. You're not stuck here like we are!" he yelled at her.

Brandy got up and ran over to the door to call for one of the doctors or nurses to come in. Zach continued to yell while his face turned red. Even I started to get nervous at the situation.

"I want to go home!" he yelled. "I don't want to be in this place anymore!"

Dr. Smith came back into the room and stood in the doorway.

"Zach," he said calmly into the room. "Come on, step out into the hallway and talk to me."

"You're a liar!" Zach screamed back to him. "You said I was going home this week! I don't want to talk to you! I'm done talking with you!"

"If you don't come out of this room, I'm going to have nurses and security come in and get you out, and you're going to be put in the cool-down room."

"Go ahead and bring them!" he yelled back. "I'm so freaking tired of this bullcrap and dealing with this place! I want to go home now!"

With every second Zach talked, the more fired up he got. He got angrier by the second, and his face was getting a darker-red color. He started breathing heavily as he continued to yell at both Dr. Smith and Brandy. He looked like he was going to explode and hurt himself or someone else if he didn't calm down. The more I watched, the more it upset me. Looking at him yell the way he did started breaking my heart. I stood up and walked up from behind him and placed my hand on his shoulder.

"Zach," I said in a very soft voice.

"What?" he yelled as he was turning around and looked at me. I was quiet for a moment. Seeing him like this started to upset me to the point I was holding in tears. I was lost for words on what I was going to tell him, so I said the very first thing that came to my mind.

"It's okay," I said in a cracked voice softer than what I said before that. "Zach, it's okay."

He started to calm down, his heavy breathing starting to go back to normal as the redness left his face.

"No," he said as tears started flowing from his eyes. "No, it's not, Larry. It's not okay. I was supposed to go home this week." He started crying, which made it difficult for me not to. I tried my best to stay strong.

"It'll be all right," I said. He got even more upset, and I put my hands on his shoulders as he wiped away tears that were coming down his face. Dr. Smith came into the room and stood behind him.

"Zach," he said. Zach turned around from me and looked at him. "Come on, let's go talk about this in your room. I'll go find your consoler too."

"All right," he said and started nodding. "All right, we can go. I'm sorry."

Dr. Smith smiled as the two of them walked out of the room. Dr. Smith followed him out of the room. I looked over at Lucy and Sarah, who looked as shocked as I did. A couple of tears made their way through my eyes, and I wiped them away before Lucy or Sarah noticed. I could tell they were just as upset about seeing Zach like that as I was. That whole situation was a mess. Brandy came back into the room and sat at her desk.

"Thank you for doing that," Brandy said. "You know you didn't have to. It wasn't your place, but I'm sure that really meant a lot to him."

I shook my head and sat back down next to Lucy. Above coming here, above working on my menus or even my meals, nothing was worse than seeing Zach break down like that. That was one of the worst things I went through so far with being here for treatment.

We were silent for the rest of the class. I didn't want to talk about it, and after what happened, it sure wasn't an appropriate time to ask Lucy for her number or if she liked me. I just sat and continued reading while Lucy worked on her art for school. Besides a few comments about the school and Brandy coming over to help Sarah with her schoolwork, no one said a word.

"How did seeing Zach like that make you feel?" Christina asked me. She came to get me right after lunch. A group was going on in the adolescent room, but I didn't mind missing it to speak to her. I'd started to enjoy my meetings with her. We sat in our normal spots in my bedroom. My hands were folded on my lap, the sun shining from outside running across my face, as did the lights.

"I must admit, it was pretty bad," I said. "No, let me rephrase that. It was god-awful." I looked out my bedroom window into the parking lot and the church steeple in the distance. Dean told me that there would be days that I'd love being here and that there would be days where it would feel horrible. I didn't know what to feel. I felt bad for Zach, but I didn't know how bad I should feel. I understood his pain, but I wanted him to stay, too, if he needed additional help, before he went home.

"I have to be honest," I said. "Seeing him like that, just exploding, it reminds me of one night that I did after I left my therapist's office. I exploded because I knew I was hurting myself and I overheard my sister crying. For a moment, I felt like I was in my sister's shoes."

"This might sound like a stereotypical therapist question, but how does that make you feel?" she asked.

"Trapped!" I said. "Like I have all these emotions building up inside of me and I don't know what to with them. Honestly, it makes me feel triggered. Knowing that all these things around me are going on and I can't do anything about it. That was one of the things that made me feel triggered to begin with." I talked fast, shaking my head in confusion, not knowing if she'd even understand.

"I get that," she said. "I know exactly what that feels like. That trapped feeling, it's from holding in everything. Now, let me ask you, what should we do when we feel this way?"

"I normally bottle things up," I said.

"That's not good. When something like this happens, we must find ways to cope. With your eating disorder, for example, when those feelings you have come up, you need to find different ways to deal with them. We call them coping mechanisms." She reached into a folder she had and pulled out a sheet of paper and gave them to me. On the sheet was a list of different activities in different categories. From group projects to different hobbies, to distractions, to spiritual and religious activities.

"What I want you to do, for therapist homework, if you will, is pick three of them," she said. "During our next meeting tomorrow, we can discuss them. Prayer is on the list, and I'm sure that will be one of them. Sarah enjoys painting. Maybe talk with her about that?"

"I've noticed Lucy draws too," I threw in while looking through the list.

"Keeping in mind that we want you to focus on using coping mechanisms, there's something your team and I have decided I should talk to you about." I looked at her, intrigued, while waiting for her to continue. "We have to up your meal plan," she said.

I could feel my heart drop in my chest a little at hearing her say that.

"Okay?" I said. I avoided making eye contact with her as I tried to think it over. I knew they would have to sooner or later; I just tried to push it off and avoid thinking about it the best I could.

"It's okay to be upset, Larry," she told me. "Almost no one handles this news and is 100 percent okay."

I still avoided looking at her. I thought it would hide the fact that I felt upset. Obviously, it wasn't working. I felt nervous and scared. I didn't want to move up. I felt my heart beating quickly all over again. She leaned in closer to move my attention back to her.

"That's why I need you to focus on finding different ways of coping," she said. "And look at it as a positive. If we up your meal plan and we can push through this, we can take you off bathroom observations."

I smiled at the excitement of hearing that. That was something I'd been looking forward to.

"That's the smile I'm looking for!" Christina told me. "You can move through this. I know you can!"

I smiled even more and looked back at the sheet of paper and skimmed through different ways I could cope.

"One more thing. I called your sister," Christina said. My attention went off the paper and went straight to her.

"How would you feel about a family therapy session this Saturday morning? I normally don't work weekends, but it's hard to find a time that works with both your sister and her husband from where they're both first responders. Bless them."

"That's fine with me," I said, nodding.

"Great!" she said, standing up. "Remember, work on picking which coping mechanisms you want to utilize. You'll be surprised how far down the road to recovery they'll bring you."

As she left the room, I looked over the list again. This could really encourage me to start praying more.

As I continued to work my way through this program, I noticed one of the things I needed to do was pray. I'd been reading the Bible a lot, but I needed to find time to pray alongside that. Another one I thought about was reading. I looked over on my nightstand at the short stack of books that were sitting there. My Bible was one of them. Alongside that were books I got from groups so far and a copy of *Mere Christianity* by C. S. Lewis. There were other things on the list, like a distraction when negative feelings came up. The list said I could try focusing on something else or distract myself from what I felt. I didn't understand how that could help me in recovery, though. Shouldn't I try to focus on my feelings and work through them instead of pushing them off? *How is that any different from bottling things up?* I thought to myself. I put the list down on my bed and started to walk toward the group room. I was sure whatever group they were in was over or just starting to wrap up.

On my way back to the group room, I started to think about Zach again, and Lucy as well. I still wanted to tell her how I was starting to feel. I also wanted to check in on my friend to make sure he was okay. As I continued my way back to the group room, I thought of words I could try to say to the both of them. *Prayer can start here,* I thought to myself. *Father, give me the words to say,* I said in my heart. When I made it to the group room, I saw that Lucy and Sarah were there. I walked into the group room and sat down on the other side of the couch as Lucy.

"Have you seen Zach?" Sarah asked. I shook my head no. Sarah was watching *Breaking Bad* on Netflix.

"I'm surprised they even let us watch this," I said.

"They don't," Sarah said, laughing. "Matt comes in and yells at me to change it every time he comes in the room." Around that time, Zach walked back into the group room.

"Hey, guys," he said in a calm voice.

"Hey!" I yelled. Sarah got up and went over to hug him. Zach came over and sat in the recliner. "How are you feeling?"

"I must admit, a lot better now." He looked at all three of us. "I'm really sorry about what happened and going off like that."

"Don't be sorry. It's really okay," Sarah told him.

"It's not that I hate the staff here or hate anyone here, it's just I was really ready to go home," he said, looking around the room. "This isn't my first time here."

"It'll be okay," Sarah told him.

Zach threw a fake smile on his face. "Thank you," he said. "You know, this is my second time here. I was here once, got out, and was home for a few months before having to come back. Dr. Smith saw my weight drop and thought I was relapsing again, and that was why he made me stay an additional week."

We were all silent for a moment.

"You know what the problem with recovery is? It's easier here. When you're in treatment, you have nurses and doctors watching you constantly. I mean, they put cameras in our bedroom and watch us sleep, for God's sake. They watch us eat our meals, they go through our trays when we're done, and you even have to earn the right to use the bathroom without them listening."

I nodded in agreement as he talked. He was right.

"Then you get out," he continued. "You complete the program, you leave here and go home. Then suddenly you don't have the nurses watching you eat or even to make sure that you do eat. No one is there to watch you use the bathroom or watch what you do in there. What you do when you get out of treatment is fully up to you and what you've learned and accomplished while you're here."

"I've never thought of it that way," Sarah added.

"They say when you get here, you're starting the road to recovery. But treatment to me feels like the red light on the road. True recovery doesn't start until you get out of here and can make your own decisions again," Zach said.

"That's deep," I added. Zach turned his head and looked at me, trying not to laugh. "What's so funny?" I asked.

"That's what she said," Zach said, breaking out laughing,

"Welp! There's that fifteen-year-old humor I was missing over the last couple of hours. With that, I'm going to the bathroom before the next group starts," Sarah said while walking to the door. When she got to the door, she turned around and looked at us. "And your girl just got off bathroom obs too!" she added, throwing up peace signs, which made me laugh even more.

"I gotta do the same," Zach said. He stood up and followed her out. After that, it was just me and Lucy. *Breaking Bad* was still playing on the TV. I wasn't paying attention to it, and I doubt she was either.

"Well, today has been…how do you say it?" I said.

"Let's say different," she said, chuckling.

I smiled again, I found it was easy to smile when I was around her. The longer I was around her, the easier it got to smile. It was just me and her again. I wanted to tell her how I was feeling toward her before the others got back, but I didn't even know where to begin or what I could say. I looked over at her. She looked beautiful, even in just a T-shirt and no makeup on. She looked breathtaking. I couldn't stand another day without at least bringing it up.

"How do you feel about me?" I asked while trying not to stutter on my own words or chock on my tongue.

"What was that?" she asked. She looked confused yet happy at the same time. Sort of like she knew where I was going with this already.

"What do you think about me?" I asked. "I must admit, I'm starting to like you, a lot. I know we're in here, though, and this isn't the place for, well, romance. But I was just wondering what you thought about me."

She smiled at me and pushed her hair back from one side of her face to behind her ears. Her cheeks started to blush, too, which made my heart start beating quickly.

"I like you too," she said. She was silent for a moment.

"So where do we go from here?" I asked. "I mean, we are…well, here."

"You're right," she said. "At least until both of us get out of here. It's not like we can go out on a date or anything while we're here."

"We should focus on ourselves right now. Maybe revisit this when we both get let out of here?" I replied to her.

"Agreed!" she said, nodding. "I'd like that a lot," she added, smiling. I smiled back at her and turned my head back to the TV and *Breaking Bad* playing on it. Sarah had had the volume turned on low so Matt couldn't hear it from down the hall or the nurses couldn't hear it from across the hall in the nursing station. I looked at the TV and back at her. Then back and forth. And it hit me.

"Or we can go on a date here," I said.

She started laughing a little bit at the idea.

"How do you propose we manage that?" she asked, still laughing.

"You and me, we can have somewhat of a date here. We can wear the nicest clothes that we brought here. I'll come knock on your bedroom door and walk you down to the group room during visiting and cell phone hours. We can have a movie night here, just the two of us," I said.

She went from laughing to smiling and blushing again.

"That is one of the weirdest ideas I've ever heard," she said. "But honestly, it's one of the most adorable ones as well." She continued to smile as she thought it over. My heart continued to beat out of my chest.

"Let's do it!" she said.

"Great!" I said with a sigh of relief and a big smile on my face. "So I'll pick you up from your room. This Friday at seven o'clock?"

"Sounds good!" she said while breaking out laughing. "And you better not be late."

"I'll look ahead on my phone and see what the traffic looks like. Hopefully, it'll be fine and the weather holds up," I said. She started laughing even more. The sound of her laughter was enough to give me goose bumps. My whole day just went from stressed to one of the best days I had since I started coming here. I tried to say something else, but before I could, Matt stuck his head in the room.

"You know you guys aren't supposed to be watching this!" he said. I looked at him, confused, before turning my head back to the TV, with *Breaking Bad* still playing. Lucy got a smirk on her face and turned her head from him.

"I'm sorry," I said, smiling. I went up and got the Xbox controller and shut the TV off.

# CHAPTER 21

I moved my checker piece across the board. Brandon came to visit me that Thursday night, the night before my movie date with Lucy. I asked him if he could bring up one of my button-up flannels for the night, and he did. Over the week, Lucy and I had grown closer to each other. We'd stayed up in the group room during phone hours again to talk and to get to know each other better. Her dad came to visit yesterday night, and Brandon came to visit me tonight. Brandon and I were playing checkers in the hallway so Dean could join us. We would have played in the group room, but Dean wasn't allowed in the adolescent group room, or us in theirs.

"I'm telling you, man," I said while moving my piece across the board, "this girl, she's…I don't even know how to put it into words."

Brandon smiled, taking his turn in the game. "I'm glad to see you're starting to feel happy again," he replied. I nodded. "I'm serious, bro. I am happy to see that you're happy. Tell me more about her."

"For one, she has an interest in God. She struggled with her faith a little when she first got here. I did too, though. We've been working on that together. She wants to go into social work. She loves walks on the beach, going to the movies, and she laughs at all my jokes."

"She laughs at your dad jokes?" Dean said, laughing. "You need to marry her already."

"I like this guy," Brandon said, pointing at Dean while Dean laughed and pushed his hair back. "His jokes are rather bad, aren't they?" Brandon asked, laughing alongside Dean.

"You gotta keep working on it," Dean said. "I know this really isn't the best place to start a relationship, but I would be lying if I said I never have seen it happen. I've seen very strong relationships and friendships form out of places like this."

"Just don't forget the real reason you're here," Brandon said. "I want you to continue working on getting better. Now, I don't have any issues with you dating, obviously. But don't forget the original reason you're here."

I started thinking about Lucy and getting better. My meal portions going up did really bother me at first. I almost skipped the meal completely. The look of the size portion scared me, and Lucy and Sarah could both tell it was overwhelming me and making me upset. It took a lot of praying, and I picked up the coping mechanism of journaling too. But I started to cope with it better and started completing meals again.

"You look healthy," Brandon said. I didn't why that upset me, but it did. It upset me a lot. I started overthinking before he started talking again. "I can tell you're upset. I didn't mean it that way," he said.

"I know you didn't," I told him. "Don't worry about it."

"I'm not saying you look fat or anything like that at all," he said. "You just look…healthy."

I threw a smile on my face. I looked up the hall and saw Lucy at the nursing station. The nurse got up and started following her to her room.

"That's her," Dean said, nodding. Brandon turned around quickly and turned back to us.

"She's a pretty girl," Brandon said. "Go for her, bro, and king me," he added while moving his checkers piece across the board.

I looked down at the board, between thinking of Lucy and my meal plan I forgot we were in the middle of a game.

# CHAPTER 22

I was not much with dressing up; I was never that good at it. Even at my sister's wedding—the suit I was wearing looked worn, and my hair was not as neat as it should have been. But that night, I did the best I could. I had a black-and-red flannel I tucked into my dark-blue jeans and put my sneakers on. I wanted to look my best for Lucy even if it was just a movie date night in the group room. The nurse passed out cell phones, so I had to use my camera as a mirror to make sure my hair was in order, since I still was on bathroom observation and couldn't use a mirror.

I stood outside Lucy's bedroom door; I couldn't get her flowers, so I learned how to make a paper one on YouTube very quickly. I took one deep breath and tapped on her door. When she walked out, I smiled and slapped my hand over my heart. She looked beautiful. She was wearing a long-sleeved sweater and blue jeans as well with short heels on.

"Madam," I said.

"Hey," she said, laughing a little. "How was the traffic getting here?" she asked jokingly.

"Pretty bad," I replied. "I got stuck at a hospital on the way over here."

She laughed jokingly and pushed my shoulder a little. Her smile made it impossible for me not to smile.

"Shall we?" I asked as I handed her the paper flower. She smiled at it and said she was going to put the flower on her bed and went back in. When she came back out, I nodded, and we walked to the group room. For obvious reasons, we couldn't hold hands or hug before we started going. I was disappointed, but I still made the best of it. The group room was empty, and that was exactly what I was counting on. We sat in the same spots we did before, on opposite sides of the couch. We had to try to keep the nurses' attention off us.

"Is there something specific you want to watch?" I asked as she picked up the Xbox controller to go through Netflix.

"Let's watch the first movie suggestion they give us," she said. I went with it. It didn't matter what movie we watched for me; my focus of the night was on her. She opened Netflix, and the first movie that popped up was called *Creep*.

The movie was one of those found-footage movies about a guy claiming to be dying and he hired a guy to film him for the day so his unborn son would know what his dad was like. But you learned toward the end of the movie that the guy wasn't dying and turned out to be a serial killer who was luring this guy to his house. The main character sure did earn the movie its title. By the time the movie ended, I was over 100 percent positive I'd have trust issues for a while.

"Well," Lucy said as the movie ended, "that was… well…"

"Interesting?" I asked sarcastically.

"That's the word," she said, starting to laugh. I sat up in the seat I was sitting in and turned to face her better now that the movie was over.

"Why did you come here?" she asked after a moment of silence.

"What do you mean?" I asked. "Why did I come to this unit?"

"No, I mean *here* with me. This movie, this 'date.' I think it's cute, and it really means a lot to me. But why?" she asked. "Why now and not later on, when we both get out?"

I was quiet for another moment. Truth be told, I didn't know why, and I was not sure if I needed to know.

"I don't know why. It's just…we're both in a tight spot right now. I could tell from the moment we met, and you didn't want to talk that you didn't like that you had to be here. I just knew that I wanted to do whatever I could to make being here more enjoyable for you. Yeah, we could have waited until we got out to do something like this, but I wanted to see you smile now."

She started to smile and blush as I was speaking.

"That was a good answer," she said.

"Why'd you say yes?" I asked.

"Well, to be honest, you're kinda cute," she said, laughing. "And I thought the idea you had was really cute. To be honest, even though the movie scared the death out of me, I thought this was a lot of fun."

"There's no one else I'd rather be here with," I said.

Sarah and Zach at that time came into the room.

"Cell phone time is over!" Sarah said. "We have another hour before they tell us it's bedtime!"

Zach sat on the recliner, and before Sarah could sit between Lucy and me, Lucy moved over and sat next to me. Lucy turned, looked at me, and smiled. Sarah grabbed the remote and turned *Breaking Bad* on again since Matt had already gone home for the night. Now that all of us were in the group room again, I doubted the nurses would be paying attention to just Lucy and me. I put my hand on the couch, and I offered her to hold it. She looked down at my hand and put hers into mine. Suddenly, my world seemed at peace.

All four of us sat in the group room and told one another jokes and made one another laugh to the point that our sides hurt. It was at that moment that I realized I wasn't on this journey to recovery alone; I never was. I was making lifelong friends, friends that could relate to what I was going through, friends that could give one another advice and pick one another up on our bad days and encourage us on our good. Even though I was two hours away from home, with these guys I felt like I was home.

I thought at that point Sarah knew that something was going on between Lucy and me. Sarah looked over Lucy's lap and saw the two of us holding hands. She smiled at us and nodded.

"Nice," Sarah said and gave us a high five. It made Lucy blush, and it made me laugh. As time passed, we laughed and talked as *Breaking Bad* played on Netflix. Lucy and I sat hand in hand until the nurses came in and told us it was time to go to our rooms. But suddenly, for that hour of all of us together with one another, the world didn't seem too bad, and us sitting as friends, I forgot for a moment that I was in an eating disorder unit. It wouldn't have surprised me if they did too.

I started to walk Lucy back to her room to wrap up our "date" for the night. We walked slower than we should have because all I knew was that I didn't want the night to end. I didn't want to leave the group room, and I dreaded the moment that I would have had to let go of her hand.

"I have to say, this has probably been the most unique date I've been on," she said. "Thank you for spending the time with me." We got to her door, and she stood outside her room in front of me. I knew we couldn't touch; it wasn't even a good idea to hug. The last thing I wanted was for one of us to get in trouble with the staff here for becoming too intimate with each other.

"I really had a lot of fun tonight," I told her. "You are absolutely amazing." She wiped some fuzz off my shoulder.

"You're so sweet to me," she said.

"I want to do this again," I said. "Outside of here. Maybe when we both get discharged from here, we can go to a movie, or maybe dancing. Anything you want."

"There's nothing I want more," she told me; she looked a little disappointed, though.

"Are you okay?" I asked her.

"I'm fine," she said. "It's just…I'm a mess right now. I do like you, and I do want this to work. I just don't understand why you'd want to be with someone like me."

"Because I don't care about your past. Anything you've done, God forgave you for the moment you asked. All I care about is where we go from here and making you happy. You are a wonder," I told her. A couple of tears rolled down her face, which she wiped away. Lucy then looked up and down the hall both ways to make sure a nurse wasn't watching us. When there wasn't a nurse standing in the hall, she walked closer to me and threw her arms around me and kissed me on the cheek.

"Thank you," she whispered.

"Anything for you," I whispered to her.

"Now, go to bed," she said, laughing a little bit. "You have family therapy in the morning."

"You're right," I said, laughing. "Good night," I said, and she turned around and started to walk into her room.

"Good night, hun," she said softly, turning around while she turned her bedroom light on. "Let me know how tomorrow goes with Christina and your family."

"You know I will," I said, and with that, I turned around and started walking back to my room.

When I got back to my room, I got one of the biggest surprises I could imagine on top of how great tonight was. The sign on my bathroom door that read "Bathroom Observations" was taken down, and there was a note on my bed.

*Larry,*

*Congrats! I normally tell you this in person but couldn't catch up with you, but you're off bathroom observations, and I took you to level 3, meaning you take walks outside the unit tomorrow with your sister if you choose to. Congrats on your hard work!*
*—Dr. Smith*

*Yeah!* I yelled in my head, and I threw the letter on my nightstand. I went over to the bathroom door, and it was unlocked. It felt amazing to finally be able to use it without a nurse watching. Between being off bathroom observations and the night I had with Lucy, I felt so excited I didn't know if I'd ever be able to fall asleep. I thought the night Lucy and I started talking was a night that made me happy. That didn't compare to how happy I felt and the way Lucy made me feel tonight.

My heart was fluttering, and I felt so many positive emotions that it was overwhelming. I got down on my knees at my bedside and prayed to God and thanked Him for the night and what He blessed me with. I jumped up and crawled into bed after. No one in this hospital, staff, patient, visitor, or student alike, was happier than me that night.

# CHAPTER 23

I sat in my room, waiting for Emily and Blake to arrive. I hadn't seen them since the morning I was brought here, so I was more than excited to see them. A few staff members were cleaning and organizing the group room since we were having the therapy session in the group room. After a night like last night with Lucy and my friends, I felt excited and happy. I was excited to spend more time getting to know her better. I felt excited to spend more time with my friends. I sure was excited to see my sister. I had a long way to go in recovery, but whatever God had in store for me, I was excited for it.

"Larry," a voice said over the speaker in my room. "Your family is here for your family therapy session. Please come down to the group room."

"Yes, ma'am," I said with a smile. I didn't think she could have heard me, though. It didn't matter. Today was already off to a good start.

I completed breakfast, and Sarah, Zach, and Lucy wished me luck afterward. *I got this,* I told myself and started for the group room.

Emily and Blake were standing by the nursing station, signing in. The moment I saw them, I couldn't help but feel overfilled with joy. I walked down the hall a little faster than normal to greet them.

"Emily!" I said a little louder. When she saw me, she ran over and met me, and we hugged each other.

"I am so happy to see you," she said. She stood up on her tiptoes to reach and kissed me on the forehead.

"We've missed you, bud," Blake said, walking over to meet us. I threw out my hand to shake his, and he grabbed my hand. "Forget that," he said, and he pulled me over to him and gave me a hug too.

"I missed you too," I said.

Around that time, Lucy and Sarah were walking down the hallway. Since we were about to use the group room, they had permission to sit in the adult one.

"Is this your family?" Lucy said.

I turned around and saw the two of them. "They sure are," I told them. Lucy and Sarah introduced themselves to them. Zach followed behind them a couple of moments later.

"You have an amazing brother," Lucy told Emily before they started walking away. "Have fun, Larry," she added, turning around, waving. As they walked away, Blake turned and pointed at her nonchalantly and smiled.

"Don't look at me like that," I said sarcastically. His smile turned into a smirk. "It's a good story."

"I knew it!" Blake said. "You don't have to explain."

"What can I say?" I said with a laugh. "I put the *stud* in *Bible study*."

Blake gave a loud laugh and pushed my shoulder.

"That's the humor we've been missing," he said. "I'm really happy to see you happy again."

"You look so good," Emily said. Christina came out of the group room and waved us over. We were still down the hall from where Emily ran to meet me when we saw each other.

"Larry," Emily said as we were walking back. "Before we go in there, I need you to try to relax. Whatever way you feel will be okay. I just need you to try to stay calm."

"What are you talking about?" I asked.

"Please promise me you'll at least try when you go in there," she said. At that point, I thought I had a feeling about what she was referring to. I walked down the hall a little faster and looked through the window of the group room. I saw him. My dad was sitting on the couch in the group room, talking to Christina. My eyes got big, and I took a deep breath in and started backing up until my back was against the nursing station.

"No," I said. "No, no, no."

"Larry," Emily said. It was too late; I already started walking back down the hallway away from the group room. I didn't think my dad saw me. His back was to the wall that connected the group room to the hallway. Christina did, though, and she came out of the group room and started chasing after me.

"Larry," Christina said, "are you all right?" She grabbed my elbow, and I turned around and looked at them.

"I'm not going in there," I snapped. "You said this whole thing was going to be with my sister and Blake. You never said a word about…"

I started shaking my head back and forth and pointed back at the group room.

"You never said a word about him being here." I breathed in deeply. "Why is he here?"

"It's not her fault," Emily said. "She tried to discourage me from bringing him, even asked if he'd not come in. Don't blame her. It was my idea."

"Why?" I asked. "What would make you think bringing him here was even close to being a good idea?"

She was wordless and couldn't think of anything. Christina couldn't either.

"Do you not realize that he's one of my biggest triggers and one of the reasons I have the problems that brought me here in the first place?"

"That's why I brought him," she said. "If you two can work past the bitterness and hatred you have for each other, maybe it can help you move on, maybe it can help you heal."

I started shaking my head no, trying to keep tears from coming out again.

"I don't know if I can do this," I said. Right at that moment, bad thoughts started going through my head that this would go horrible and he would ruin the progress that I'd made so far. If he even cared enough to be here, why wouldn't he come out to meet me? He must know I was out in the hallway. Why couldn't he have come out to meet me?

"Bud," Blake said, coming over to me. "No one blames you for being upset. I know how hard this is for you. But this could be the first step to you and him working things out. I know you love him, and that's what you really want, isn't it?"

Emily came over and wiped a few tears off my face.

"Okay," I said, nodding. "All right, let's try."

"Attaboy," Blake said, patting my back. "Attaboy, come on," he added, and we started walking toward the group room.

The closer we got to the group room, the more my heart began to sink. My heart started pounding so fast I had trouble breathing. All I could think of was him cursing at me, backhanding me, punching me in the gut. It all came back more vividly than what was actually in front of me. I walked into the group room and walked across to sit in a chair directly across the room from him.

"Larry," he said in a serious yet scratchy voice. "It's been a while, hasn't it?"

"Yeah," I replied in a soft voice. "Yeah, it has." I looked at him. It felt like looking hate in the face. His black hair was cut a little short and pushed to the side. He had stubble on his face that was starting to turn gray. For all the drinking he did, he was in great shape, though. He sat with his arms crossed over his hoodie. My heart at this point felt like it sank deeper in my chest than I did in the chair. Emily and Blake sat on the couch, and Christina came in and pulled up a chair from the table and sat in front of the television.

"Well," Christina said, "this is going to be the first family therapy session you guys have together. I just want to go over a few rules." As she went over the normal confidentiality laws, I began to pray in my heart that this wouldn't end up in total disaster. My dad sat with his arms crossed, looking down at his legs, which he had stuck out in front of him.

"There's one more rule I want to add," Christina said. "I understand that there may be unease in the room right now. So I want everyone to respect one another. No yelling, no talking over one another. Understood?"

We all agreed.

"Okay," she said. "Now, I know you guys probably don't have much experience in family therapy, so the first question I want to ask everyone is, What do you guys want to get out of this? Is there anything specific you want to go over?"

There was a moment of silence in the room.

"I'm just looking forward to seeing Larry home," Emily said. "I miss his old self and seeing him as that happy-go-lucky kid I watched grow up."

"I fully understand that," Christina said. "You want to see your brother healthy and happy again. Well, today I want to talk about just that. I want to go over what the eating disorder is, how it's affecting Larry, and what you guys can do to help him when he gets out to make the home a good environment for his recovery."

Emily smiled and nodded in agreement.

"I don't see how that's going to work," my dad said. Christiana gave him a puzzled look. "I don't see how you're going to help us give him a better place at home to recover when all he did was hide this from everyone. To be honest, I didn't know he had this problem until he was hospitalized for it. No one even told me he was here until the other day."

"Would you even care if I did?" I spoke up and asked.

"So what I'm hearing is, you're a little upset that all this was kept secret from you?" Christina asked him.

"Someone should have told me," he said. "That's all I'm saying."

"I tried to!" I said, a little louder. "I tried calling you and asking if you think I should go, and you never answered or called back, I might add."

"One call. One call?" he said and started to raise his voice as well. "Well, obviously, my opinion doesn't mean much to you since you didn't want me here to begin with."

"Guys," Christina interrupted. "What did I say in the rules? This is not a place to argue and yell at one another. Please." I looked over at Emily and could tell she was starting to get upset and was probably feeling that bringing him here was a mistake. Blake looked uncomfortable.

"Let's start with going over what an eating disorder is," Christina said. "Do you guys know much about this topic?" she asked.

"I don't," Blake said. "From my knowledge, someone stops eating because they think they look obese?"

"In some cases," Christina said.

"I'm getting treatment for bulimia," I told Blake. "With me it's different, because instead of not eating, I try but I fail sometimes, and I end up binging food instead and then vomiting it all up."

"Why?" my dad said. I could hear mockery in his voice. "What, do you think you're fat or something?"

"It's not just that," I said while trying to remain calm. "That plays a role in all this, but there're other things too. Like, after everything that happened after Mom died and, well, what happened between us, I was using it to cope. I felt like the only thing I had control over was my weight."

"Oh!" he said. "So it's my fault? Is that what you're saying?"

"Dad, please," Emily said. "He didn't say th—"

"Let me tell you something!" he threw in. "I took care of my family, and I did my best as a parent, and you told me I would do nothing but drink myself to death. I didn't blame anyone for my drinking. But now look where you're at!"

"Dad," I said, trying to get him to calm down.

"You know what your problem is? It's not an eating disorder! It's you constantly blaming everyone else for your problems!"

I tried telling him again that I wasn't blaming him for anything, but he continued yelling. I could smell beer coming off his breath. If he was drinking already this morning, he was still drunk from the night before.

"You're almost an adult!" he yelled. "You need to learn how to grow up and be a man! Take some responsibility for your life for once instead of blaming your mother, me, and some petty failed relationship for your problems!"

I sat in silence.

"You didn't think I knew about that?" he asked. "Your sister and I talk way more than you think. She told me about your breakup, which confuses me on why she didn't tell me about any of this."

I was at a loss for words, trying to hold back everything I wanted to tell him.

"Besides that advice, I don't see what more you could want from me."

Finally, I broke down and started yelling back at him.

"I wanted you!" I yelled, standing up. "I wanted you to be a dad when I needed you to be! I needed you to show you care about your son, your family! I needed you to put your bottle down and actually talk to me! Was that too much to ask for? If you'd looked at me, or if you actually cared about me, you would have known something was wrong with me, like everyone else did!"

"Enough!" Christina yelled, and we both quieted down. "I will not tolerate you guys yelling at each other anymore! You two can either be mature here or this session will be over. Am I understood?"

I sat down, tears flowing down my face again, with a mixture of feeling heartbroken and abandoned. I felt the same way I did the night all this went down. I leaned back in my chair and looked across the room at him. He looked like a big mixture of drunk and tired. I could tell he didn't want to be here just as much as I didn't.

"Dad," I said, looking over at him as soft and calm as I could, "the night you threw me out, right on top of Mom's death, I don't think you understood how much that crushed me. Please, I'm not blaming you for any of my problems. I just want to work things out with you. But I just don't get it."

"What don't you get?" Christina asked.

"You say you talk to Emily a lot. I've never seen you two argue the way you and I do. I've never even seen you treat her the way you treat me. I just want to understand why you treat me so badly, why you only treat me badly. Did I do something wrong to you?"

He sat there quiet. He looked down and leaned forward. He looked ashamed of himself. He kept looking around the room but didn't say a word. This made me feel even more upset with myself. I started wiping away tears as Christina passed me a box of tissues.

"Randall," Christina said, looking at my dad, "is there anything you'd like to say to Larry?"

"Son," he said. I didn't think I'd ever heard him call me that. Maybe that was a good sign. "Your eyes are green."

"So?" I asked in a puzzled voice. "Mom's eyes were green."

"Mine are blue," he said. "Your hair is a dark-brown color, while both your mother and I have black hair."

"I don't understand," I told him. "What are you getting at?"

He looked right past me and looked out the window. He didn't say anything.

"Your mother was Christian right before she died, but she wasn't always that way," he said.

"Right before she was pregnant with you, I caught her having an affair," he added. "At that time, she'd been drinking. She said she didn't fully remember how it all went down, but that didn't change anything. I was going to divorce her, but she would have done anything to save our marriage, so she went to church to 'get right,' if you would."

I sat speechless; at this point, I knew what he was getting at. I stood up and walked farther away from him over to the windows and looked outside. He kept talking.

"It didn't change the outcome of anything," he said.

"What are you trying to say?" I asked with a cracked voice.

Emily sat in the edge of the chair, looking as speechless as I did. He sat and shrugged his shoulders.

"You do all this 'eating disorder' crap to have control?" he said. "I drink to forget. You want to know why I treat you so bad? It's because every time I see you, I see him. Every time I see you, it's a constant reminder of…" He choked up on his words.

"A reminder of what?" Emily asked.

He looked over to her and then back to me. "Larry, I'm not your dad," he said.

I shook my head and turned around so I didn't have to look at him. I put my hand on the window and looked down. I was trying to shake my head no and pretend I wasn't hearing any of this. This couldn't be true. It couldn't. Even Christina was lost for words, it seemed. Emily started crying, and she came over and put her hand on my shoulder.

"Maybe it's not your fault, but the only way I could stay sane is to treat you like it is. After all, the situation would have been done and over with if you weren't born," he said.

"Shut up!" I yelled, turning around. "You're a liar. None of that is true!"

"Oh, it's not?" he asked. "How are you going to tell me that? Don't live in denial, boy."

"This entire life of mine has been a lie?" I asked calmly. "You lied to me my entire life about being my dad?"

"I had to for your mother," he said. "We worked things out the best way we could away. I kept my mouth shut."

"You both lied!" I said.

"I said I did because of your mother!" He started getting a little louder. "I don't see how any of this is on me!" he yelled.

"It's on you and Mom! Please, if you were going to lie to me about being my dad, you could have at least done something to try to be one! What's the point of lying about being my dad if you weren't going to act like one and treat me like a son?"

He didn't say anything. For the first time in my entire life, he was speechless.

"Even if you're not my biological dad," I said through tears and anger, "you were the closest thing I had to one. So maybe you need to ask yourself why you couldn't be a man and fill that role."

Christina stood up and walked over to me.

"Ge away from me!" I yelled, and I stormed out of the room. I raced down the hall despite the "no running" rule. I didn't care at this point. On top of everything I'd had to deal with, this dragged me down more emotionally than anything else.

"Where are you going?" my dad said, stepping out into the hallway after me.

"Hey," Dr. Smith said to him. "Come with me."

I kept speed-walking down the hallway to get to my room as fast as I could. Emily stepped out into the hallway and started chasing after me.

"Larry!" Emily yelled.

I stopped and turned around.

"Why would you bring him here?" I said in a stern voice, trying not to yell at her. I knew it wasn't her fault. "You see what happens when we are together? Nothing good." Pure anger was on my face. She didn't say anything. She just looked at me with tears flooding over top of her eyes. After a few couple of minutes of awkward silence, she threw her arms around me and started crying. I couldn't take it anymore. I broke down and started crying and started to fall to my knees. Emily came down to the floor with me.

"This is too much to handle," I said. My head was resting on her shoulder. We sat there in the hallway, crying and hugging each other. I didn't know what was harder for her, finding out I wasn't her full biological brother or seeing me break down the way I was in the middle of the hallway. I'd broken down in front of her, but never anything this bad before. I couldn't handle this anymore. I couldn't deal with it. I couldn't deal with seeing Emily this upset either.

"I'm not good at this," I said through my tears.

Blake finally came over and took a knee next to us. A couple of nurses came down, too, to check if I was all right. I let Emily go and sat down and leaned against the wall. I spread out my legs on an angle and put my elbow on my knee and my fingers over my eyes, wiping the tears from them.

"Larry," Blake whispered to me. "What happened in there was terrible. I mean, it even upset me. But its's nothing we can't work through."

I breathed heavily through my nose, and one of the nurses handed me a couple of tissues.

"We got to get up from this," he said. "We all love you more than you will very know. This isn't going to change anything."

"It hurts like crazy," I said.

"I know it does," he replied, "but we got to keep pushing. We got to keep fighting. Come on." He stood up. He reached out his hand to me, and I took it. Blake pulled me up to my feet, and the second he did, he threw his arms around me and started patting me on the back.

"Attaboy," he said. "Attaboy."

Christina came over and explained that she was going to cancel the rest of the family therapy session for the day. She told me I could feel free to go back to my room if I wanted to. Emily and Blake could have a few minutes with me alone, but after that, they would have to go. She wanted to come in and talk with me after they left.

"Thank you," Blake said to her, and he threw his arm over my shoulder and I threw mine over his.

"Let's go, bud," he said, and we walked back to my room.

I still felt horrible. I felt like my entire world had just completely stopped. That if I was on the road to recovery, I just got hit head-on by a truck. But I knew my sister and Blake were always going to be there for me. I turned around and looked again before turning the corner and saw him standing out in the hallway, talking to the nurses and Dr. Smith. They were probably questioning him on what happened in there between us and what was said. It didn't matter. At the end of the day, I didn't care what was said between us. I didn't care if we were biological or not. He was the closest thing I had to a dad, and even if it was not by blood, he still should have done a better job.

When we got to my room, I walked over and got in bed. I sat up and continued to look at the door. I had a false hope in me that he would come in and say he was lying or that he was at least sorry for what was said in there; I knew I would if he came in.

"Are you okay?" Emily asked.

"No," I told her. Blake asked if there was anything he could do for me.

"Keep on praying for me," I said with a fake laugh.

"You got it," he said. He came over and gave me a hug. Emily followed over and hugged me too and kissed my forehead. "If you need anything, please call," she whispered. "I'd do anything to help you. I love you."

"I love you too," I said.

With that, the two of them left and I was alone in my room again. I lay back in bed and closed my eyes. Christina would be here any moment to talk, and the last thing I wanted was to talk about this. I cried into my pillow again. I buried my face into it. I felt so tired that after a couple of moments, I fell off to sleep.

There was a knock on my bedroom door. It startled me and woke me up. I looked at the clock to see I was only asleep for about ten minutes. I wasn't asleep too long, but it was long enough to make my hair messy. I sat up in bed and rubbed my eyes to try to fully wake myself up. Before the door opened, someone poked their head in.

"Hello?" a voice asked.

"Come in, it's fine," I said, standing up. It was Bill from the chapel. "Hey! How've you been?" I asked, reaching out my hand to shake his.

"I'm doing fine, Larry. It's nice to see you," he replied. "Come let's have a seat." I went over and sat on the couch, and he pulled up a chair in front of me and sat down.

"What brings you here?" I asked him through my heartache. A ten-minute power nap helped my mind in better order, but it didn't take away any of my heartbreak. Seeing him sure was a pleasant surprise.

"Well," he said, "I'm hoping you could tell me. I got a call from Christina. She said she couldn't see you like she planned because she was already on overtime. She wouldn't be able to see you until Monday. But she knew I was here and said that you 'could benefit from a chaplain's visit.' Is everything okay?"

"I'm fine," I said. I didn't know who I was trying to convince, him or myself. I failed at both. He looked at me with a face full of doubt. I definitely failed at trying to convince him.

"You want to know the most ironic thing about Christians?" he said. "They're the biggest liars. The same thing for church. More lies are told in church than anywhere else in this country. If you don't believe me, just go to any Sunday-morning service and ask someone, 'How are you doing?' They always say what you're saying: 'I'm good' or 'I'm fine.' You want to know what's funny about that?"

"What's that?" I asked.

"I'm a chaplain at a hospital, son," he said. "Not everyone here can always be 'good' or 'fine. So when I ask people how they're doing and they give that answer, I'll ask them what I'm about to ask you. Larry, how are you really doing?"

I sat in silence; I was amazed at his response.

"I just found out my emotionally abusive dad is the way he is because he's not really my dad," I told him.

I could see his smile fall of his face; he wasn't even involved in this situation, and it even upset him.

"I mean, he was always abusive toward me. I'm not as upset as I should be because of that reason, but I spent my entire life believing one thing just to find out something totally different. I don't think I'm going to be the same after today."

"Why not?" he asked me.

"Since I got saved and since I came here, I've been praying and trying to find out where God's taking me, and I'm trying to find out what plans He has, but I don't think I've heard anything from him. But now, I just don't see why God will do all this to me. I keep crying out to Him, and all I get in return is silence. What do I do with that?" I asked him.

He stood up and walked over to my nightstand and grabbed the Bible that was sitting on top of it and came back, flipping through the pages.

"How familiar are you with the Israelites in the wilderness?" he asked.

"Not too familiar," I said. "I haven't read much of the Old Testament yet."

"Let me read you scripture out of Exodus," he said. Bill started reading about the Israelites walking through the wilderness. God used Moses and just delivered them from Egypt, and they were walking through the wilderness to the promised land. They were hungry and thirsty. Overall, it was making them fed up because they thought they were better off in Egypt. They were getting ready to stone Moses and turn back to Egypt when God provided them with food to eat and water to drink. After he got done reading, he closed his Bible and handed it back to me.

"I don't like taking scripture out of context," he said, "but I do want to make this point for you. The Israelites spent their entire lives in captivity. God came and saved them from it, though, and was going to bring them to the promised land. None of them had been to this land before or had even seen it. But God still promised to bring them to it. He took them through the wilderness. Are you with me so far?" he asked.

I nodded.

"They were walking to a destination they'd never been to before. Through a wilderness that scared them," he explained. "But God still provided for them. Even if they were being stiff-necked. You're on a journey to recovery, Larry, and it might be scary, it might be uneasy, but I haven't been through a fraction of the trails you've been through, so I don't know how you feel. But on your way to your promised land, God will provide for you."

I smiled at him, and for the first time today, it wasn't a fake smile. I needed to hear what he told me.

"Thank you," I said while trying to not get emotional again. He leaned forward and patted me on the shoulder.

"Anytime, buddy," he said, and he stood up and started walking to the door. I sat on the couch in silence.

"You seem to have a heart of a servant," he said, turning around, looking at me. "Use that. Jesus said He didn't come to be served but to serve others. I know there's not much you can do here, but try to go out of your way for someone. Make someone smile or laugh. Tell someone they're loved."

"I will," I said, smiling, and he walked out of my room, closing the door behind him. I stood up and was getting ready to use the bathroom when I noticed a piece of paper lying on the floor, with "From Lucy" written across the top of it. She must have slid it under my door while I was taking a catnap. I picked it up and read it.

*Larry,*

*I hope everything is okay. I heard yelling from the group room all the way down to my room. You know, if you ever need to talk, I'm always here for you. Meet me in the group room after lunch. We can talk then.*

*Love,*
*Lucy*

I should try to get my mind off Dad, or the closest person I had to a dad. Bill was right; I should try to make someone smile or laugh. I knew what I wanted to do. I would go completely out of my way to make Lucy laugh. I would walk to the ends of the earth if it meant seeing her smile. I went back and sat in bed, thinking of ways to do that. The night we started talking, she said she was sad because she was missing out on her prom and missing out on graduation because she had to be here. Maybe there was something I could do. I should at least try it. I sat in my room, trying to figure something out, planning on giving Lucy something that would make her happy. I kept thinking over my options and what I could do. Then finally it hit me. I stood up and ran over to the door, and when I opened it, Lucy was right about to knock on it. She almost scared me. We stared at each other for a couple of seconds in silence.

"Hey," I said, smiling at her.

She walked over and hugged me. "I'm so glad to see you're okay," she said. I put my arms around her gently, trying not to tear up. I didn't care if nurses saw us, and I didn't care if we'd get in trouble for touching each other. At that moment in time, I didn't want to let her go. She let go and backed up a little bit.

"What happened?" she asked. She was talking fast. I could tell she was worried about me. "I heard screaming from the group room all the way down the hall to my room. Finally, when I stepped out in the hall, I saw you on the floor surrounded by staff. Sarah and I were coming down, but we got told to turn around. We started freaking out because we didn't know what was going on, and it just got worse and—"

"My dad came," I said in a soft voice. "It's just…it's never easy when he's around."

"What happened?" she asked.

"He's not my dad," I said, trying to not get emotional in front of her. "He admitted to me that we weren't blood-related, and it turned into a whole fight and mess."

She put her hand over her mouth in shock. "Larry, that's terrible," she said. "I'm so sorry."

I told her it was okay. She quickly hugged me again.

"Is there anything I could do?" she asked me.

"I want to see you happy," I told her. "Aside from whatever happened with my dad, aside from the situation that we're both in, above it all, I want to see you happy."

She looked at me and blushed.

"I want to give you a night out," I said. "I know you said you were going to miss prom because you had to be here. I know you said you were going to miss graduation because you had to be here. I want to give you a night to make up for all that. Everything that you said this place is going to keep you from, I want to make up for it all." She looked so happy when I said that. Her face lit up, and it made my stomach feel like there were butterflies in it.

"Is there something that you had in mind?" she asked while holding a smile on her face. "I know we can't do much while we're in here, but it doesn't matter to me as long as it's with you."

"Let's try to get a pass for next weekend," I said. "If we can both get a pass and get the chance to leave the unit for the day, we can spend the day enjoying whatever downtown Princeton has to offer." She looked at me. She looked surprised by the idea but intrigued by it too.

"That sounds wonderful," she said. "Is that something you really want?"

"All I want is to see you happy. And I want to do whatever I can to be the one that makes you feel that way." She went in and hugged me again.

"Step one is getting a pass for next weekend," I said.

# CHAPTER 24

I met with Dr. Smith and Christina the first thing Monday morning, right after breakfast. After the incident Saturday morning, they didn't want to be hesitant in seeing me. They thought that both of them being there would be a good help for me too. I didn't go outside that morning, but judging by the window fogging up and the fresh blanket of snow covering the ground outside, I could tell it was a bitter, cold morning. Most of the weekend, I planned on things Lucy and I could do if we got the pass together. I looked into a couple of restaurants for dinner and a place we could possibly dance at. I wanted to give her the prom she wanted, even if we couldn't go to her actual prom.

The last couple of days were horrible when it came to dealing with what happened with Dad. I kept trying to wrap my head around everything that happened and just couldn't. I prayed. I talked it over with Brandon and Emily. I felt like I was hit by a train. I stayed up late in my room Saturday night. I cried, I prayed, and I went over all the what-ifs. I kept trying to think of how Saturday could have gone better, the things I should have said. I shouldn't have let him see me get upset; it felt like I had given him exactly what he wanted.

"I want to compliment you," Dr. Smith said. "After that family therapy session, at least from what I was told happened, you had a moment, but the nurses said you were calm the rest of the weekend. They mentioned you stayed in your room a lot, but considering the news you've learned, I don't blame you."

"Can I be honest with you?" I asked.

"I hope you have been," Dr. Smith said, laughing. That made me laugh a little too. "There's a smile. But continue," he said.

"It doesn't bother me that he's not my dad. After everything he's said to me and the things, he's put me through, that's not what bothers me. He was so abusive and distant it was never like he was my dad, anyway. It's the fact I've been lied to about it my entire life. What bothers me more is that I'm not fully blood related to my sister. But what bothers me the most is how he told me," I explained. "He came to my therapy session without me knowing and says something like that when I'm already dealing with the trauma he's given me. How could he think adding on to it would be a good idea?"

"Hey, Larry, I get it," Dr. Smith said.

"Would you say you felt betrayed?" Christina asked.

"Betrayed and lied to," I added. "By both my dad and my own mother too. I guess she just didn't want me to have a bad picture of her is all."

They both looked at me in silence for a couple minutes. Dr. Smith looked over to Christina and back to me.

"There's another reason we wanted to meet with you," he said. "With what you're going through with your family, I think it would be beneficial and healthy for you to get out of the unit for a little bit. I'm sure by now you're familiar with what a pass is?"

I tried not to show it on my face, but my emotions on the inside started to light up. He was going to give me a pass for this weekend. Things were starting to look up. I did, though, ask him for more details on what it was.

"What a pass is, well, a pass," he said, chuckling. "You would be able to leave the unit for a day. Typically, you would leave a little before lunch starts, or right after, and you get to leave until that night. You can be gone as short as you want but would have to be back before lights-out at eleven."

"I would just leave?" I asked.

Christina went into more details on it after Dr. Smith. She said I couldn't leave by myself. Since I was seventeen, my sister would have to come sign me out or have someone that she approved of come sign me out. *Okay,* I thought to myself. *That might complicate things a little, but they could still work out with Lucy.* Right away, my mind began to wonder about Emily signing me out if it happened. Would it be okay if I saw Lucy outside the unit during?

"Give your sister a call sometime this week," Dr. Smith told me. "Let me know what she thinks about it, if she's able to come get you for one of the days, and get back to me on that before Friday morning."

"Yes, sir," I said, nodding.

After they left, I tried my best to not over celebrate. *I got the pass!* I screamed in my mind repeatedly. For the first time since Saturday morning, I felt so overwhelmed with happiness it was impossible for me to not smile. We weren't fully there yet, though. Lucy still had to get her pass, and we both would have to be able to find someone to not only take us out but also be willing to let us see each other. My first part was done, though.

I sat in the group room after lunch. Lucy got pulled by Dr. Smith for their daily meeting right after lunch, so I sat down hoping for her to say she got the pass when she got back. I sat in the group room next to Sarah, watching *SpongeBob SquarePants* on the TV. Matt was getting so annoyed by telling us to stop watching *Breaking Bad* that he took the Xbox away from us for a few days.

"We should have watched Bob Ross," Zach said.

"What?" Sarah said, laughing.

"Don't 'what' me," Zach said, smirking at her. "Bob Ross is amazing and on Netflix. Watching him wouldn't have gotten the Xbox taken from us." They stared at each other with straight faces for a couple of seconds before Zach broke out laughing. It was dumb and simple things like that that always reminded me how much fun I had when I was around those two.

Lucy came in a few moments later.

"I got a pass for this weekend!" she exclaimed. Sarah congratulated her. Lucy was extremely happy, so happy her face started to turn red. She walked over the couch and sat down next to me and clapped her hands.

"I must admit, you seem overly happy about getting a pass," Sarah said. "Big plans?" Lucy looked at me and back at her and laughed a little. Sarah nodded at us and smiled. I think she figured out what we were planning at that point.

"Where are you two going?" she asked.

"I'm not sure yet," I said. I had looked into a couple of different places to take her. I did find out, though, that downtown Princeton was expensive, and I'd been out of work since the first time I went to the hospital. "We'll figure something out," I said, smiling while looking at Lucy.

"You two are cute," Sarah said.

"And disgusting," Zach mumbled. Sarah laughed and punched his arm. My only problem now was finding a way for us to get outside the unit together. That was step 2.

I sat in the group room after dinner, waiting for Lucy to show up. We made plans to meet at the end of the day so we could make a plan on what we wanted to do this weekend. I was nervous but excited at the same time. I didn't know what we were going to plan, which was what made me nervous, but the fact it was working out so far was what excited me. Everything raced in my mind, from what I wanted to wear to where we were going. The amount of thoughts racing into my mind seemed to be racing my heartbeat. That seemed to happen a lot every time I thought of her. When she came to the group room, she was hiding her phone in her hoodie. During phone hours, we weren't allowed to leave our room with them. The moment she walked in, my heart fluttered.

"I have everything worked out," she said, coming in and sitting down. "I just got off the phone with my dad and my friend Megan. My dad is going to give the staff here permission for Megan to pick me up and take me off the unit." That was fast; I didn't even think about who to ask to take me out, Emily, Blake, or Brandon. I thought they'd all be willing to help me out with this. I just didn't know which one I wanted to ask. I didn't want them to drive over two hours just to sign me out, then go home. That would be a waste of their time.

"So how would we work this out?" I asked. "I know you said you live far away too. I don't want to take advantage of our friends by having them drive up here to sign us out."

She agreed with me.

"We still have a few days to think on it," she said. "I'm still trying to figure out what to wear."

I didn't know what I was going to wear either. I didn't want to wear the same T-shirt and jeans I'd worn since I'd gotten here. That was all I brought, T-shirts, jeans, and a hoodie. I thought it over for a couple more seconds, then it hit me.

"We can spend the day getting ready," I said. She looked at me in confusion. "Hear me out. What if our friends pick us up and we go out with our friends for a couple of hours? We spend some time with them, we can go hang out with our friends, and we can go wherever we need to get something to wear, then have them drop us off at a meeting spot around dinnertime and the rest of the night can be ours. I can even have my friend Brandon drive my truck up, and he can ride back with his girlfriend so we'd have transportation after they drop us off."

"That's a great idea," she said. She thought it over a little more. "That's actually a really good idea." So far, it was a good idea; I just had to call Brandon to get him on board. I didn't think he'd have any problems doing it; I just didn't want to make promises without being 100 percent sure he was on board.

"I'm going to call my friend now," I said. She said okay with a beautiful smile on her face, and I walked to my room as fast as I could without a nurse telling me to slow down until I got in my room. I called Brandon, and he answered almost as soon as I pressed the Call button.

"My dude!" he shouted over the phone.

"Big man!" I yelled back. It just hit me that moment in time the dumb ways we would greet each other. The thought was funny. "Hey, I have an important favor I need to ask you," I said.

"Sure, bro, what is it?" he replied.

Right there, I explained to him everything. I told him about the family therapy meeting, I explained to him what happened with my "dad," then I went in and explained to him about how I got a pass for this weekend and how I planned on using it to take Lucy out. I asked him if he could help sign me out for the day.

"I still can't believe what I'm hearing," he told me. "Your dad isn't really your dad?" he asked. He sounded as shocked as I did, and as shocked as Emily did at that. Looking back on my childhood, it all started to make sense. How he randomly started drinking and channeling his anger toward me. He must have found out when I started growing up. When he saw the differences in us, he must have found out something was off. I didn't understand how the rest of us didn't see it.

"I agree with them fully," he said. "We got to get you out of there to get some fresh air. I can pick you up Saturday at noon?"

"That would be great," I said. "One more thing. Could either Lilly or Tanner drive my truck up here? I'm going to need something to drive that night when it's just me and her."

"Are you kidding me?" he asked sarcastically. "Of course. I've been wanting to get a date night with Lilly for a while. So we will both drive up there, have our own date, and we can take the truck back down if you want."

"That would be perfect!" I exclaimed.

Brandon went back after that and asked me about my dad. He asked what I planned on from there and how things would be different when I got home. Honestly, I didn't think about that at all, but when he asked me about it, I thought about it and I didn't think things would be much different. I didn't live with him anymore; we didn't even talk after he threw me out. The only difference now would be that I knew he wasn't related to me anymore. I'd be okay.

When I walked back into the group room, she sneaked up behind me and grabbed my shoulders. I turned around quickly because it scared me, and she laughed.

"I got approval from my dad and my friend Megan. Megan is coming to get me on Saturday," she said. "How did it go with Brandon?"

"We're all set!" I exclaimed.

She clapped her hands together, and in that moment in time, I didn't think I'd ever seen her as happy as I did. She seemed so excited and thrilled about it, and seeing her happy made me happier even more. I knew this week was going to go by slow. How excited I was about something! I knew this week was going to drag by, but it would give me time to focus on my health and recovery and give me time to plan on where I wanted to take her. My heart was beating so fast from excitement I could hardly stand still.

"It's almost time for bed," a nurse said, poking her head into the group room. I was surprised they didn't know that something was going on between us.

"I'll walk you to your room," I told her. Suddenly, one of my perfect nights came to an end.

The week went by surprisingly fast. Emily felt bad after what happened last week, so she came by to see me, both her and Blake. I explained to them what I had planned, and Blake congratulated me on progressing through the program and getting to recovery despite what happened with Dad.

Zach went home on that Wednesday too. Dr. Smith stayed true to his word and only made him stay a little bit longer and decided he was healthy enough to go home and to try to stay healthy and to continue his road to recovery. The night before he left, he came over to my room, and even though it was against the rule on patients being in each other's rooms, we sat in my room and had guy time. He told me about his concerns with going home, and even though he was more than excited about it, he was nervous about falling again and having to come back a third time.

"I know it'll be difficult," I told him, "but I know you can handle this. I'm proud of you." I patted his shoulder. After that, I prayed with him. Before we could talk any more, a nurse told him he wasn't allowed to be in there and he had to go back to his own room. Before he left, I gave him my number so we could stay in touch. After that, it was just Sarah, Lucy, and me. Everyone else in the unit and everyone who was coming in after that were all adults. As Dean mentioned before, sometimes there were days I loved it there, and other days it felt like nothing but pain. I was happy to see Zach go, but I missed him.

The rest of the week, I felt sad. I just missed having a guy friend closer to my age around.

# CHAPTER 25

I sat in the group room, waiting for Brandon, and I was excited beyond understanding. I was wearing jeans, my flannel from the movie night I had, and a hoodie. Blake gave me some money, while he and Emily helped me buy nicer clothes while I was out. The plan was to hang out with Brandon and Lilly, go to a mall or something to get the nicer clothes, and Lucy and I were to meet at a restaurant at 5:00 p.m. Lucy's friend Megan already came and signed her out, and they were gone. It was just me, waiting for Brandon. I saw Lilly and Brandon walk up to the nursing station, and I ran out to greet them.

"Hey!" I yelled at them. Lilly turned around, and her jaw dropped.

"Oh my goodness!" she said, and she walked over and hugged me. "Look at you! You look so much better!" she said. Brandon came over, and I gave him a hug too.

"My man!" he said, laughing.

I walked over to the nursing station and signed out. Brandon signed, too, and showed the nurse his ID so they knew it was him. Then we headed out. As we walked through the lobby toward the front door, excitement filled me. This was going to be the first time since I'd gotten here that I was going to walk outside. When I did, it felt amazing. The cold winter air smacked me right in the face, and even though it was freezing out, it felt like heaven. I took a deep breath and enjoyed the Princeton fresh air and took it all in before Brandon and I got in the truck.

"I missed you so much," I said.

"Missed you too, bro," he said.

"I'm talking to the truck," I said, laughing, while Brandon punched my shoulder.

"Okay, so what's the plan?" Brandon asked.

"There's a mall about five miles away from here," I said, if my phone was correct, and Brandon pulled it up on his GPS. "I'm going to go there to get clothes. Maybe a button-up shirt and some dress pants. I'm meeting Lucy at a restaurant called Princeton's Night Sky. It's an Italian restaurant. Their reviews talk about how romantic it is."

"Okay, so I'll drop you off there. What time should Lilly and I be back at the hospital for the truck?" he asked.

"We have to be back by lights-out at 9:00 p.m.," I said. "So if you guys can stay out that late, I'd more than appreciate it."

"That's completely fine," he said. "Anything to help you two out. You guys deserve this."

When we got to the mall, Lilly pulled in behind us and I explained the plan to her so we'd all be on the same plan. The first thing I did when we got inside was go look at clothes. It was pricey, but I bought a plain white button-up shirt, black pants and shoes, and a heavier suit jacket since it was cold outside. I sat in the dressing room, no shirt on, looking at myself in the big mirror that hung on the wall. For a moment, I felt happy. I was outside the unit; I was getting a taste of what it would be like when I got discharged. Then I really got a good look at myself, and I didn't like what I saw. I knew I was gaining weight back on while I was in treatment—that was one of the objectives of going—but I felt disgusted with myself. I didn't like what I saw in the mirror. I started to get worked up and sad. *Distract yourself,* I told myself, but it wasn't working.

Coping with this was hard, even harder knowing there wasn't a nurse or staff watching. I sat in the changing room for a few minutes, crying at the change I saw in myself. I knew it was good; it had to be good. I just didn't feel like it was. I felt a few tears run down my face, which I wiped away before Brandon came and knocked on the door to check on me.

"Are you okay? You've been in there a while?" he asked, and I wiped my face again.

"Yeah, I'm fine!" I told him. Nevertheless, the clothes I picked out fit, so I got them together and headed out. "These are fine," I told him. I said a quick prayer in my mind and heart, and we headed out and I bought them.

For the next few hours, we walked around the mall, got a cup of coffee, and explored what the place had. The MarketFair mall was small, but overall, it was beautiful. It had a sunroof on it, and the walls were a warm tan color. It was a beautiful place. We walked around, and Brandon got Lilly a bracelet until it was time to head over to the restaurant. I ran to the bathroom and got changed into my dress clothes. This time I looked in the mirror and saw someone completely different. I thought of Lucy and the night we were going to have, and I felt happy. I hurried back out to the truck to meet Brandon waiting for me.

"You look great," Brandon said to me. We were sitting in the restaurant toward the back. My chair was facing toward the entrance of the restaurant. Brandon was sitting in the chair next to me while Lilly waited in the car for him.

"Thanks, bro," I told him, looking at him.

"I know you were upset at the mall in the changing room."

I looked over at him, and my eyes got big.

"We've been friends our entire lives. I know when my best friend is sad." He chuckled.

I laughed a little with him.

"The point is that you've been doing great. You've been working hard, and I can see it. I can see it in the way you look and how you've been talking. I want you to drop everything right now," he explained to me. "What your dad told you, everything you've been through, just for the night. It's you and Lucy. Enjoy it. You deserve this."

"Thanks, bro," I told him and smiled at him. "I can't express how much it means to me that you did this for me."

"You'd do the same for me," he said. Lucy walked in the restaurant, and the host up front pointed her toward my direction. She looked perfect. From the way she did her hair to the dress she was wearing. If I were wearing a heart monitor, I knew it would show my heart skipping a beat.

"Go get her, buddy," he said while patting my back. He stood up and started walking toward the exit. Lucy came over, and I was lost in her eyes for a moment before I snapped back into reality.

"Hey!" I said, standing up to greet her. I hugged her and pulled out her chair for her to sit. When I sat back down, I couldn't help but stare at her.

"Are you okay?" she said, smiling.

"Yeah! I'm sorry," I said, picking up a menu. "It's just… you look beautiful."

She blushed before saying a thank-you.

"You look handsome yourself," she told me. Lucy was wearing a dark-blue dress that went down to her knees. It had a white strip around the waist. Her hair was straightened and pulled back into a ponytail. This was the first time I'd seen her with makeup on, and it brought out her beautiful green eyes.

"How was your time with your friend?" I asked her. She told me how Megan brought the dress she was going to wear to prom with her, so she already had that. So instead of clothes shopping, they went to get their hair and nails done so she would look nice for tonight.

"It was nice to have a girl's day before coming here," she said. "With everything leading up to me having to come here, I didn't get much of that."

"Is there a reason?" I asked. She seemed a little nervous about answering the question. "You don't have to answer that."

"No," she told me. "It's fine. Megan and I played field hockey together for school. I passed out once in a game because of the anorexia, and they said I couldn't play anymore. I got embarrassed and wouldn't talk much."

"I understand that," I said. "I felt the same way. Embarrassed, I mean. Brandon's girlfriend came up with him so they could drop my truck off for me. So I didn't get to have much guy time. She's fun to have around, though."

When the waiter came to take our order, I could tell that Lucy was nervous about ordering. I was too. This was the first time since I went to treatment that no one would be monitoring me eat. I didn't know how to handle it. I kept thinking to myself that this wouldn't be any different from eating at the unit. The only difference was, there was no nurse watching. I could do this.

"I'll have chicken strips and fries," Lucy ordered. I ordered the same. It was simple and easy. It would be a good place to start as my first meal off the unit. If we could get through this, then we could have an amazing rest of the night. There was a place called the Love's Café up the road that had a small outside floor I was going to take her to after this.

"What's the plan when you get out?" she asked. "What do you want to do when you go home?"

"It'll be nice to get back to school," I said. "I've been looking at what I want to do when I get out of high school, but I'm not sure yet. I've been jumping around from choice to choice."

"You should be a pastor," she said. I smiled and shook my head. "No, I'm serious. You'd be a great one."

I asked why she thought I would.

"You care about people," she said. "That's just one. Secondly, you have a testimony to share with everyone. I know you're still working on it, but God has brought you through so much and you could help a lot of people with that story. I know you're still new to the faith, but you know a lot for someone who is new to it. Maybe it's something to think about over time. If you're being called to it."

She made a good point. Since I'd been here, I'd read through the entire New Testament. I never thought about being a pastor until it got brought up in the unit. It was something I would have to think about for the rest of the school year and while looking at colleges. But the thought of it was on the table. Speaking of the table, right after that was when the food got there.

"Here we go," the waitress said putting the food down. "Is there anything else I can help you with?"

"No thank you," I said.

"Enjoy your meal," she said, and as she walked off, I was about to say, "You too!" but caught myself before I said it. I caught it fast enough for the waitress to miss it, but not fast enough for Lucy. She started laughing at me.

"I'm so awkward," I said in an even more awkward voice while trying to not laugh at myself. I looked down at my food, and that nervous feeling came back to me. I started to take deep breaths to try to prevent myself from getting worked up. I put my arms on the table and looked down at the plate. The food smelled good. *I can do this,* I told myself. *I can do this. I can do this.*

Lucy grabbed my hands with hers.

"Hun," she said. "It's okay. We're in this together."

I could tell she felt nervous too, but she smiled at me, and even if the smile seemed fake, for a moment I didn't feel alone. I knew God was always with me and I was never alone, but it felt even better knowing I had someone else by my side. I couldn't help but smile back at her. Between her beauty and that she was there for us to support each other, I couldn't help but smile. She squeezed my hands a little tighter and asked if I'd say grace. We prayed over the food and started eating. I kept talking to her and not focusing on eating to keep myself distracted. It was easy to do so. The sun going down over the city outside with a mixture of the restaurant lights brought out her eyes.

We sat for almost over an hour, talking about things from our passions to how we grew up, to some of the more embarrassing yet funny moments of our lives. She never stopped amazing me at some of the things she would tell me.

"I have a passion for working with kids and people our age," she said. "I want to work with kids and help them with things they can't control or feel like they can't control. That's why I want to do social work."

We had similar passions. I wanted to help make the community a better place in any way I could. Whether that would be from taking criminals off the street in law enforcement or even being a pastor and helping the community, like Lucy mentioned. Either way, I had a passion similar to hers. By the time my food was over, I got so lost in having a conversation with her and focusing on her that the fact I was eating never crossed my mind. The waitress came and left the bill for us, which was cheap.

"I had a really fun time," she said. I did too. It was only dinner, but I had more fun with her than I did in months, and I let the tip I left the waitress show it.

"The night's not over yet," I said, smiling at her. "How would you feel about leaving the truck in the parking lot and taking a walk?"

"That sounds amazing," she said.

The lights in the distance from the group home was nothing compared to what downtown Princeton really looked like. Between the old buildings and the snow that covered the ground, mixed with the streetlights, it looked like something that came out of a book. It was a wonderland. Princeton's nights sky was absolutely mesmerizing. The sidewalk was packed, but it felt like it was only Lucy and I walking the streets, hand in hand. She looked cold, so I took off my jacket and gave it to her to wear.

"Where are we going?" she asked over top of the city noise.

"You'll see soon enough, love," I said.

She smiled at me. She must have smiled at me over a hundred times since I'd met her, but this time it felt different. Every horn honking and person talking seemed to vanish. Right there, she was all I could see. She was all I could want to see. She was the only person I could want here in this moment. She was mine. We rushed through downtown Princeton, laughing and moving with the motion of the city. Everything seemed perfect. Between her, this city, and being out of the unit, I could feel my heart melt in the cold weather.

We got to the café, and I took her through and ordered both of us a cup of coffee. I walked her over to the table.

"This place is called Love's Café," I said. "This is the first place I wanted to come to when I saw it." I took a sip of my coffee.

"Why here, though?" she asked. "What made you want to walk all the way down here?"

"Come with me," I said, and we walked out back to a dance floor. Outside, there was already a crowd of people on the dance floor. Other couples slow-dancing outside underneath the stars. There were heat vents that blew to keep it warm enough. She looked at it all in amazement. I walked up behind her and put my hands on her shoulders.

"I want to give you the prom night you said you couldn't attend," I said. "What good is a prom night without dancing?" I asked. She turned around and looked so happy she was getting ready to tear up. I held out my hand, and the moment she grabbed it, I spun her out onto the dance floor and pulled her close to me.

"I didn't know you could dance," she said surprisingly.

"I don't, to be honest. I'm just winging it and hoping I don't embarrass myself," I said. She laughed and put her head onto my chest. We danced—well, tried to dance—on the floor for a couple of minutes before I let her start leading, because I didn't know what I was doing.

"I'm sorry," I said. She laughed at me again.

"Don't be," she said. "I think it's cute. At least you're trying." She taught me a couple of moves and then asked for me to try.

"There you go!" she said as I started getting it. I had never slow-danced before. After Anna left, I didn't think I would be going to prom with anyone either. I continued moving along with the music, with her between my arms. She still had my jacket on.

"Can I ask you something?" she said.

"Of course," I told her.

"Why would you do all this for me?" she asked. "What made me so special that you would go so far out of your way to do all this?"

"All I want to do is to see you smile," I said. "From the moment we met, you were quiet. I knew I had to do whatever I could to make you happy. From staying up late and thinking of dumb jokes to tell you in the morning, to spending my day planning this. I knew if it made you smile in the end, it would be worth it."

"But why?" she said.

"Because you're worth it," I said. Her face started to turn red and blushed as an old George Strait song said, "It's more than the wine." She leaned up and kissed me on the lips this time.

"I love you," she said and put her arms around me. I continued moving with the music.

"I love you too," I said.

The Princeton night sky was perfect enough, but having her in my arms made it even better. I thought getting out of the unit would make me happy. I thought seeing the world from the view of Princeton would be what made me smile, but it was more than that. I could travel the entire world, I could go wherever I wanted in the world, but it wouldn't be enough to make me happy, because my world was in my arms.

After we danced and got back to the truck, we had about ninety minutes before we had to be back at the unit. The walk back to the truck was peaceful and quiet. The city started to calm down as most of the college students went back to campus and almost everyone started to go home. There were still a lot of people in the city, but not nearly as many as there were. It was a quiet walk back to the truck. We held hands, and she walked close to me. She seemed to move in closer the further we walked to the truck. I made sure I opened the truck door for her and closed it for her, then got in the driver's seat.

"Tonight was fun," I said. "Beyond fun."

"I couldn't have asked for a better night," she said. "We danced, we had dinner, we had a romantic walk through the city. I can't think of anything else better to do. I don't think this could have been better than prom. Thank you so much," she said. I started to lean in to kiss her, and she met me halfway. As we started kissing, thoughts rolled through my mind. I pulled away from her a little.

"How would you feel about making one more stop before we go back to the unit?" I asked.

"I'm up for it," she said. I did a quick search on my phone, and we drove off.

We drove up to a gray stone brick church. It was wide, and on the far end a church steeple went up and seemed to touch the sky from how high it went up. Out front read, "St. Paul's Catholic Church." I parked the truck out front, and Lucy got out with me as I approached the building.

"Why'd we come here?" she asked as I walked toward the church. I looked up at the steeple in awe as I walked closer to the church, with Lucy following from behind me.

"From my bedroom window at the unit, every time I look past the parking lot and past the tree line, this place is all I could see. It was the steeple to this church," I said. "It always helped remind me that there was still a world beyond this unit. Even if I'm not Catholic, I wanted to visit here before I left Princeton." I went over to the very front of the building and sat down in the grass and leaned my back against the building. I held my hand out. Lucy came over and sat down next to me, and I put my arm around her.

When she mentioned it was cold, I turned and held her with both my arms, and she rested her head on my chest. I'd only been in treatment for a month, but it had felt like a lifetime. I sat with her in my arms, and for a moment, the world stood still. I kissed her forehead, and she looked up and we kissed again.

"I love you," I whispered to her.

"I love you too," she said. "I'm always going to, love."

I thought I knew this all along, but I knew that I would have to do everything I could to make her happy. I would do anything to protect her. I would do anything to see her smile and laugh.

Young love moves quick. Young love is a beautiful thing, and nothing could take it away from me that night. It was dark, but the streetlights reflected off the snow and lit up the entire churchyard. It felt like I was sitting in a Bob Ross painting or a fairy tale. No one, not a college student, not a visitor, not a tourist, not a resident under the Princeton night sky, was as happy as I was.

# CHAPTER 26

Monday

"After looking over your chart for the weekend and this morning, it shows me you've done a fantastic job here," Dr. Smith said.

"I did?" I asked. It was Monday morning, and I was having a normal meeting with Dr. Smith. He pulled me from class.

"Absolutely!" he said. "See, one of the things I look at is how you do on a pass. According to your chart, you didn't lose any weight while going. You gained a little. That's a good sign. Especially after what happened with your dad. You didn't restrict or purge while you were out, did you?"

"No, sir," I said, shaking my head. "I didn't."

"I'm proud of you," he said. He looked back at a clipboard he was holding with my file on. "I'm setting your date of discharge on the twelfth of this month."

"Wait," I asked, "a week from today?"

"Yup," he said, leaning in his chair. "Larry, we are all so proud of the work you've made here. We think you're ready to give this a try."

My heart started speeding in excitement. I could hardly sit still.

"Thank you so much!" I said. "Really, you have no idea how happy this makes me!" I reached out my hand and shook his.

"You still have another week, though," he said. "Remember, things can change in a week. If I see a change in mood or weight, I could extend it like we had to do with Zach. So you have a whole week to work on yourself and your recovery. Use it," he told me.

"Absolutely!" I said with excitement. After that, he looked at the clock and made mention that it was almost lunchtime.

"Congratulations, Larry," Dr. Smith said, walking toward the door. "I'm so proud of you and everything you've overcome."

"Thank you!" I told him. I stood up and walked out behind him and went to the group room to find Sarah and Lucy before lunch started. They were both in the group room.

"I'm leaving in a week!" I yelled at them, walking into the room. They all jumped up and were happy for me. They both hugged me and congratulated me. It was amazing news.

By the time lunch was called, I walked down to the dining hall with my chin high. With Lucy by my side and the news of going home soon, nothing could take the smile from my face.

At lunch that day, I sat next to Lucy. Things seemed to be even better with her now that I could plan on what to do when I left. So far, except Saturday's date, it had been limited by this unit. Now that we would both be getting out soon, I started thinking of what this meant for us. We could start planning our relationship outside of here. I kept my hands by my side after eating, and Lucy put hers in mine under the table. My heart felt like it fluttered, and all I wanted to do was to see her in the sunlight again.

## CHAPTER 27

### Wednesday

"How do you feel about leaving soon?" Christina asked. Today for our therapy session, she decided we could use the group room instead of my bedroom. We could sit in better lighting and have more space. With the curtains pulled back and most of the outside wall being a window, the light from outside lit up the room so well we didn't even need to turn the light on if we didn't want to.

"I must admit," I said, "I've been more excited than I thought I would be on my first day here."

"How so?" she asked me.

"Well, my first day here, I thought I was just going through the motion, trying to get to the end so I could go home and return to the way things were. But what if I don't want them to?" I asked. "I mean, I've only been here a month, but this place showed me the changes I need to make. Not just in the way I take care of my body."

"In what other way?" Christina asked.

I had a few moments of silences while I thought of the best way to word it.

"In how I involve the ones I love into my life. I can't just keep hiding when I get upset from them. In my walk with

Jesus, this place has given me a lot of alone time with him and time to work on my faith. I don't know. I just…I needed to come here way more than I thought I did. It wasn't until I spent the time here working on myself that I saw that."

"You've done everything right," Christina said. "You worked hard, you overcame a lot in your life. More than anyone your age should have had to. We're all very proud of you."

I smiled while holding tears of joy in.

"Thank you," I said with a cracked voice. This wasn't going to be an end to my struggle, but a new beginning. I knew there was going to be a lot more struggles in life, even with bulimia. It wasn't going to be all sunshine and breezy. There was going to be time of struggles and nights when I felt weak. I knew that because there were plenty of nights while I was here when there were struggles. There sure were plenty of times when I felt a struggle. But being here gave me a foundation I needed to work toward recovery. With my faith and with Lucy by my side, things weren't going to be as bad. *Only a couple more days,* I thought. *Only a couple more days.*

# CHAPTER 28

Thursday

Right after lunch on Thursday, I sat in the group room, watching TV with Sarah. Lucy was in her room, working on her menus. She felt more comfortable doing them in private. I could fully understand that. Sarah and I were watching some kids show on Netflix. Matt finally gave us our Xbox back, with us promising that we wouldn't watch *Breaking Bad*. Over the last month, Sarah and I had grown a friendship that I'd hope would last a lifetime. Sarah was the first person I met when I came here, and she had done nothing but made this entire process comfortable for me. She and Zach were both amazing friends to me.

"What's the plan?" Sarah asked me. "When you leave Friday morning, what do you plan on?"

"Hopefully, to go back to school on Monday," I said. I laughed a little bit under my breath. "I can't believe that I actually miss it."

"Tell me about it. Nothing against Brandy, but I miss being around actual people and not just home instructors."

"Tomorrow night, my friends, sister, and her husband will probably do something to celebrate. I don't know what they have in mind, but they want to do something. When it comes to Lucy, all I want to do is be with her and do whatever I can to make her happy."

"That's sweet," Sarah said.

Lucy came and joined us. She came in and sat next to me right away, between Sarah and me.

"Hey, hun," I said. I wanted to kiss her but couldn't because I didn't want the nurses to freak out. I think another reason I was excited to be able to leave was so I could kiss Lucy whenever I saw her. I didn't have to worry about the nurses watching.

"Hey, babe," she said. "What are we talking about?"

"What Larry is going to do when he goes home tomorrow," Sarah said.

"You three are now part of my family," I said. "There isn't one thing I wouldn't do for any of you guys."

"Speaking of that," Lucy said, "I got you a gift when I was out with Megan the other night. I was going to give it to you when it was either yours or my last day here. I left it for you in your bedroom. Open it tonight at lights-out."

"Aw, thank you," I told her. We all sat close on the couch, all three of us watching TV. Lucy grabbed my hand and squeezed it lightly. We sat and enjoyed one another's company until a nurse came in and told us it was almost time for dinner.

"I'm going to use the bathroom before dinner," Lucy said, and she left the room and speed-walked back to her room, while Sarah and I headed to the dining hall.

"Dr. Smith says he sees me leaving in a couple of weeks," Sarah said.

"That's good!" I said.

"I was hoping to get out sooner," she said. "It is what it is, though, I guess." She looked gloomed. She didn't look like her normal, happy self.

"Are you okay?" I asked. She nodded, and I could tell she wasn't being fully honest with me about something.

"It's just…the entire time I was here, I was used to you being here, or Zach. Now it's going to just be me and Lucy. Which, there's nothing wrong with that, obviously. It's just… I'm going to miss you is all," Sarah told me. We were at the dining hall, and we grabbed our trays and walked over to the table.

"I'll stay in touch the best I can," I said. "I have your number. I'll make sure we text every night. You won't even know I'm gone. Except during the day, that is." Sarah let out a brief laugh out, and her smile returned to her face.

"Thanks, Larry," she said.

Matt came in and took a seat at the table in front where he normally sat.

"Okay, everyone!" he said. "Let's congratulate Larry on completing the program. He goes home tomorrow morning!" Everyone started clapping for me. I looked over at the adult table and saw Dean smiling at me and giving me a thumbs-up. I felt pure happiness and joy for a moment before I started looking out into the hall, though, waiting for Lucy to come back.

"We all want you to know that we are so proud of you. You have done an excellent jo—"

There was a pause in Matt's voice as his head turned.

"Are you all right?" he asked.

I turned my head where he was looking and saw Lucy standing at the end of the hall where the left side of the unit met the back corner. Both hands were grasping her chest while she looked like she was struggling to breathe.

"Lucy!" I said out loud. Her arm extended toward me. She attempted to say my name, then she took a gasp of air and fell to her knees. Lucy collapsed on herself.

"Help!" Matt yelled.

I jumped out of my chair as fast as I could and tried running to her. Matt hurried toward me and held me back.

"Larry, no!" he yelled, holding me back. "Everyone, get to the adult group room right now!" All the adults and Sarah started rushing down the opposite hallway. Matt was still trying to push me away from Lucy as both my arms were reaching toward her. Nurses and Dr. Smith surrounded what appeared to be her lifeless body.

"Lucy!" I yelled as tears flew out of my face. "Lucy, no!"

More nurses joined the effort in holding me back.

"Larry! We have to go now!" Matt yelled at me.

"Fine! All right!" I yelled. I stopped trying to get to her. At that point, I knew there wasn't going to be anything I could do about it. I started walking down the hall toward the adult group room with Matt. His hand was pressed against my lower back to make sure I didn't try to turn around and run to her again. I tried to remain as calm as I could, but I couldn't. I was shaking, and I was holding back tears. I turned around and looked one more time. The staff had her lying on her back on the cold floor as nurses and another doctor surrounded her.

"Hey," Matt said. "Come on, Larry. You can't stay here."

I looked farther down the hall and saw Sarah standing in the hallway, waiting for me outside of the group room. Her face was beet red, and a strain of hair hung in her face. A part of it stuck to the side of her eye as tears started to fall from it.

"Larry...," she said. "Did she...did she just..."

I hugged Sarah. I put my arms around her, and she cried into my chest. I put one of my hands over my two eyes. Despite the rule of no physically touching each other, Matt stood there and watched us try not to fall apart in each other's arms. After a few moments, he tapped me on the shoulder.

"Larry, we have to go in the group room," he said so softly it was almost like a whisper. "You have to have faith the doctors will do the best they can. I looked across the nursing station and saw two people who looked like doctors of some sort running down the other hall with a stretcher. My heart began to sink in my chest, and I didn't feel like I could stand anymore. My legs began to feel so weak I felt like they were going to give out from under me. They started to before Matt ran over from behind me and scooped his arms under mine.

"Okay!" Matt yelled. "I'm taking you to your room." He looked over toward the nursing station and nodded, and a nurse came over and assisted him.

"I'm sorry," I said through tears. "I'm so sorry."

"Hey, tall guy," Matt said in a sympathetic voice, "don't be. It's all right." He started patting me on the chest. They got me to my room, and I found strength to get to my bed. I lay on my beck and looked straight up at the ceiling, breathing heavily and trying to unclutter my mind.

"I wouldn't worry," Matt said. "We don't know why she collapsed. All we know is she was unresponsive. For all we know, she could be fine right now." That didn't help me. It was in the realm of possibility, but all I could think of was her in a room by herself and in pain.

"I need you to try to breathe, Larry," a nurse told me. She came over to my bed and put her hand on my chest. "Take deep breaths." It took a few minutes, but they finally got me to the point where I was relaxed enough. A nurse told me she'd come back in soon to check in on me. I looked at the clock, and it wasn't even 7:00 p.m. yet. I rolled over on my side, and my eyes started to fill with tears again. *Please, God!* I screamed in my head. *Please, God, heal her! Hear my cries for her.* I lay in bed saying everything I could think to say to God. I asked, begged, bargained, and cried. *Lucy can't die...,* I thought to myself. *Lucy can't die...*

I woke up to the sound of someone tapping next to my bed and saying my name. I tried to ignore the wake-up call, but when I realized I couldn't, I opened my eyes and saw Dr. Smith standing over me.

"We need to talk," he said. I rubbed my eyes and started to sit up.

"How is Lucy?" I asked. "Is she doing better?"

"She's stable right now," he said. "She's awake and alert. She's not doing very well, though." He looked uncomfortable and tired, like he didn't want to be here. I couldn't blame him. He should have gone home hours ago.

"Can I see her?" I asked.

"No," he said, shaking his head. "I can't allow you to."

"You have to," I said. Tears started flowing out of my eyes again, mixed with the feeling of anger. From the tears in my eyes mixed with the tears that were still in my eyes from falling asleep earlier, my eyes burned. I remembered one time when Brandon, Tanner, and I were in tenth grade and Tanner somehow got his hands on a can of pepper spray. We were sitting outside, and Tanner wanted to give it a try and sprayed it. Just being around that stuff choked me up and made my eyes burn. But the pain that the spray made me feel was nothing compared to the emotional pain and stress I was feeling right now.

"I understand you guys are close friends," Dr. Smith said. "The nurses made comments before about how close you two are. I understand, but I can't bring you over to the unit she's in. Not without her dad's permission. The only reason I'm telling you about her current state is that she asked me to and to help calm you down."

"Get his permission!" I yelled. His eyes got big, and I lowered the sound of my voice. The clock on the wall said it was almost 8:00 p.m. I wasn't asleep for too long.

"We weren't just close friends, all right? I love her. I care about her more than I care about almost anything else," I admitted, and I started to get choked up on my words. "I need to see her. If I don't and something happens to her overnight, or at all, I'm never going to be able to forgive myself. I'm never going to be able to bounce back from this." I started shaking my head. I was so upset I couldn't even look him straight in the face. I was sitting on my bed, standing up, looking down on me.

"I've lost so much. I can't lose her too. Not without at least seeing her first," I told him. I finally looked up at him straight in the eyes as I fought the tears from coming out of mine. "Please, let me see her." He looked at me in silence for a few seconds, then came down and sat next to me on the bed. My bedroom lights were still off, but the lights from outside the hallway and outside were enough to light the whole unit up.

"I have to admit something," he said. "You've impressed me."

"How?" I asked.

"You come in here completely new to your faith. New to the fact that eating disorder treatment was an option. And you've completely turned your life around. Now, everyone who come here does the same thing. But there's something about your faith that is just impressive to me. I don't know what it is," he explained. "Even after the news that the man you grew up with is not your dad, you still pressed on. If it were me, I don't think I could have."

I didn't reply. I understood what he was saying, and I appreciated it. But I still felt alone; everyone in this entire unit could come into my room right then and I'd still feel alone.

"Okay," he said, patting me on the shoulder. "Lucy's dad is on his way here. Her mom was here but left already. I'll go try to give him a call and see if he's okay with you seeing her. She got moved to a different unit."

When he left, I lay back down and continued praying in my heart for Lucy's recovery, that her dad would answer the phone, that he would say yes, and oh, how I prayed, how I prayed that if I got the chance to see her, it wouldn't be the last time.

I just needed to relax and pray. It was all in God's hands now. The more I thought about it, the more I started to stress. I started sweating and breathing quickly again. The more time dragged by, the worse it got. Sitting there in a quiet room, I could feel my heart beating inside of my chest. After almost ten minutes, Dr. Smith came back into the room; this time, he came in and turned the light on.

"You have bedhead from where you fell asleep." He had a smile on his face. "Comb it and we can be on our way."

I went to change from my wrinkled T-shirt to the flannel that I wore on our movie night date in the group room. I combed my hair down to the side, and Dr. Smith took me out of the unit. He took me to a different floor and unit of the building. As we walked, I didn't know if I should be feeling happy that I was getting a chance to see her or if I should still feel bad for the reason. Either way, I was happy that I was getting this opportunity. We walked up to the doors of the unit, and it was a unit for cardiac patients.

"Why is she at Princeton Heart?" I asked.

"She went into cardiac arrest," Dr. Smith said. "It was what made her unresponsive earlier this evening."

When we walked toward her room, I got an entirely different feel than what I got when I first walked into Six North. The place looked similar. Two halls full of rooms, a group room. But it felt different. When we finally got to Lucy's room, the door was cracked open. Before I could open it, Dr. Smith grabbed me by the forearm and stopped me.

"Before you go in, I need to tell you something," he said. I turned around and looked at him. "Lucy is not in the best condition. She's not going to look good. Right now, she's under a lot of stress. So I want you to remain calm when you go in there, all right?"

"Of course," I said, nodding.

"All righty," he told me. "Go on, I'll be back for you shortly. I'm going to go get updates from the doctors." When he walked away, he had a smile on his face, but overall, he looked sad. I took one deep breath and opened the door and walked in, closing it behind me.

"Hey!" Lucy said, smiling. She sounded thrilled that I was there. I couldn't believe what I was seeing. Lucy was on her back in a hospital gown. Her hair was pulled back in a ponytail. There were IVs going to both arms. On top of that, there were stiches in her head. She must have hit it when she fell.

"Hey, hun," I said in a soft voice. I pulled up a chair and sat next to her bed. When I did, she pulled together some strength and offered her hand for me to hold. I did without hesitation.

"Larry, I'm sorry," she cried. "I am so so—"

"Don't," I said. "Don't say it. It's okay." Trying to stop myself from crying was good at this point. There was no way I was going to be able to hold it all in.

"When they took me off bathroom observations, I did things I shouldn't have," she cried. "This is my fault."

"No," I said. "It's okay, hun. You're all right." I pulled her hand and kissed it. She was in pain, and I could tell.

"I don't remember much about what happened," she told me. "I remember feeling pain and reaching out to you. After that, I just woke up in pain here. I've been praying that you'd be able to come see me, and I'm glad you're here."

"It's going to be all right," I told her. I used all the confidence I had to tell her that.

"I don't think so," she said. She had tears rolling down her cheeks. "I overheard some of the doctors talking to my mom while she was here, and they don't think I'm going to make it through the night."

"Don't say that," I said softly. I was shaking my head no. "Don't say that. It's going to be okay. I'm not going to leave your side. I'm going to be right here for you," I was saying through my tears. The more I talked, the harder it got. Trying to talk while holding in tears got impossible.

"I don't care how long it takes. However long it takes to see you well and home. I'm not giving up on you." I wiped the tears off my face and leaned in and wiped the ones off hers. "I don't want to lose you," I told her.

She grabbed my hand again and held on to it tightly. "You never will," she said. She smiled at me while holding my hand. Just like that, her smile took me back to the way I felt the night under Princeton's night sky. The way I felt sitting against the church with her leaning on me. Just like that, just from seeing her smile.

"Larry," she said, "we have to accept the possibility that I won't be here much longer."

"I can't," I said. "Lucy, I just can't."

"You have to," she told me just as serious as she was emotional. "Larry, no matter what happens, you can't let this get in the way of you working toward recovery. Even if I can't, I want you to have a good, healthy life. Promise me that."

"I promise," I told her. "I know God is going to heal you. I have faith in that. I have faith in us. You will have a happy life. I'm going to make sure of it."

"You'd make a great pastor," she said. "And if I do make it, I'm going to enjoy seeing you accomplish that."

"When you make it," I tried correcting her. Even though we both knew I didn't know that. I was doing whatever I could to see her smile again. If this was going to be the last time I saw her, that was the least I could do.

"I was playing softball for high school," she said. "I couldn't get along with the team members, and I thought it was because of the way I looked."

I looked at her, puzzled by what she meant.

"How I ended up here," she said. "You've shared your story, but I never shared mine. It all started with trying to impress both my mom and team members."

"Mine started with wanting to get in shape like I was when I played sports in middle school," I whispered to her.

"I love you," I said.

"I love you too," she told me in a calm voice. She sounded tired, and I fully understood. I stood up and leaned over the bed and gave her a kiss. As I was kissing her, she put her hand on the side of my face, and for every moment I felt a mixture of butterflies in my stomach and soreness on my head from how sad I felt. Her soft hand on my face made the butterflies even stronger. There were a million words I could have told her, but in that moment, I was speechless. It wasn't about what I'd say for her; it was about being by her side during this time.

"You remember when I first got here?" she asked. "You tried so hard for me to start talking, and you tried so hard to show me you cared."

"Yeah, I remember," I said.

"That was when I noticed you were different from the rest of the people here," she told me. "You weren't just another patient here. You were someone I knew I could trust. From day 1 I knew I could trust you."

"I don't know what I would do without you," I said. I was starting to get emotional again. "I don't know how I'd bounce back or how I could love or care about anyone or anything. I don't know if I'd even want to. I can't lose you."

"Honey, it's because you're overthinking," she said. She pulled my hand close and kissed it again. I couldn't wrap my mind around what was happening or why it was. Everything just twenty-four hours ago seemed like it was going perfectly. Everything seemed to have just stopped again. First, my mom, and now Lucy? I couldn't let go. I didn't want to let go.

"Do you think God can forgive me?" she asked.

"Absolutely," I said. "His love and forgiveness never ends for anyone. You just have to accept Jesus as your Lord and Savior."

"Can you help me do that?" she asked. I'd seen this before; it wasn't too long ago I lay in a hospital bed, not knowing what to do. Then Pastor John came in and prayed the sinner's prayer with me. It was time I did the same thing for Lucy. I grabbed her hands, and I prayed with her.

"Jesus Christ is Lord," she cried out. I couldn't help but cry again. She meant the absolute world to me.

"Let's talk about something happy," she said. "You're going home tomorrow."

"Yeah," I said, wiping my face and putting a forced smile on. "Yeah, I am."

"Paint a picture for me," she said.

I asked her what she meant by that.

"Of the future," she said. "When I get out and we can be a couple outside of here, what will it look like?"

I took a moment to think. Lucy closed her eyes and tried her best to make herself comfortable while I talked.

"There's a spot on the beach closer to the southern part of New Jersey in Cape May. It's usually always empty. I had a bad experience there before, but it's still my favorite spot in the world. I see us there," I said. Her eyes were still shut, but she made a humming noise to show that she was still awake. "It's warm, and the two of us are walking underneath the sun. Hand in hand. The waves are crashing on the coast as the sun shows off your beautiful blond hair. We'll swim, we'll have a picnic, we'll laugh, and everything will be all right because we're together."

"That sounds nice," she said very softly. With that, she fell asleep. I was still holding her hand. I stood up and leaned in and kissed her forehead.

"I love you," I whispered. As I began to try to lift my head up, she wrapped her other arm around me and pulled me down and started kissing me again.

"I love you too," she said. I kissed her one last time and got up and walked to the door. When I turned around, her eyes were shut again, but she had a huge smile on her face.

"That's the smile I like to see!" I said cheerfully.

"Bye, sweetie," she said.

"Bye, hun," I told her. I turned around and walked out of the room, leaving the door open behind me. As I walked away, I could feel tears coming up. *Not here,* I thought. I looked over, and Dr. Smith was talking with a man I assumed to be her dad. I walked over to them.

"Hey," I said to them. The man looked over from Dr. Smith at me.

"Hello," he said. He reached out his hand to me. "You must be Larry. I've heard a lot of good things about you from Lucy." I shook his hand. He said his name was Ewan. From the bags under his eyes and his five o'clock shadow, I could tell he'd been up for a while.

"How is she?" he asked. "From where you were in there."

"She seemed okay," I said. "She could be better, but she was smiling and seemed happy when I left the room."

"We have to go back to Six North now," Dr. Smith said.

"It was nice meeting you," Ewan said, and I shook his hand. Dr. Smith started walking away, and I turned and started following him. Ewan went into Lucy's room.

"Thank you for that," I told Dr. Smith. "I don't think you'll ever understand how much that meant to me."

When we got back to my room, I walked in and felt nothing but an alone feeling. The room was as cold as the way I felt and felt as dark as it was outside. Every night since I'd been here, I always felt like I had someone here. Tonight, it felt different.

"I never do this," Dr. Smith said, "but I'm worried about you. I'm worried about Lucy too, so I'm staying here all night to keep my eyes on the both of you."

"Thank you," I said.

"I know it's not lights-out yet, but you've had a hard night. You don't have to, but I'd appreciate it if you stayed in bed and rested for the night."

I was way ahead of him. I climbed in bed and put my head into the pillow. Like I mentioned before, there had been plenty of nights since my mom passed that I cried into a pillow. Tonight was another one. *Please, God, keep Lucy alive throughout the night. Please, God,* I prayed. It was a long night, but I finally fell asleep.

## CHAPTER 29

I woke up to the light of my bedroom turning on. I already wasn't sleeping well, so I woke up the moment the lights turned on. I thought it was time to wake up, but the moment I opened my eyes, I saw Dr. Smith standing right at the foot of my bed. The clock on the wall read 2:00 a.m. Somehow, I already knew what this conversation was going to be about.

"Larry," Dr. Smith said. There were bags under his eyes, and his normally gelled and combed-back hair was a mess. Judging by the sound of his voice, he had been crying. He put his hand over his mouth for a moment. "Larry, I'm sorry," he said, shaking his head. His eyes were red.

I sat up in bed.

"What's going on," I said with a shed of hope my assumption on the situation was wrong. He wouldn't have come in to wake me up if it were good news.

"Lucy died," he said. He looked out my bedroom before he turned back to me. "She died about twenty minutes ago."

His words echoed in my mind. They replayed like a broken record. I put my face into my hands and covered the pain I couldn't help but feel.

"Larry, I am so sorry," he said. He was trying his best not to cry as well.

"What happened?" I said. I was still crying into my hands. "How did this happen?"

"Larry, these things just do," he said. "It's one of the worst parts about life and the worst part about my job. Larry, I'm so sorry." I wanted to be in denial. I really did. I kept thinking to myself I was dreaming; this wasn't happening to me again, not again. Not to Lucy. Lucy couldn't be dead. He came over to me and put his hand on my back while I cried. I hadn't cried as hard as I did since the night I left Dad's house.

"I don't know how to handle this," I said. "I can't deal with this."

"You don't have to know how to," he said. "Let it all out. Take the time you need."

So many memories flew through my mind. The night I met her, the day we first talked, and our dates. I also couldn't stop thinking about when she fell. The way she reached out to me before she did. How scared she looked and the nurses surrounding her. How would Sarah take this? If she didn't know already. Dr. Smith stayed by myside to make sure I was okay as we both cried for almost a half-hour. When I lay back down, sleep never found me. I lay in bed until the nurses came in to take my blood pressure and temperature. The *pain* never left me either.

The discharge was quick and silent. I stood up in my room, staring out the window toward the church, thinking about the night I sat there with Lucy. The sun was shining, and there wasn't a cloud in the sky. Emotional pain overtook me, and I couldn't get over what I felt inside.

There was a knock on my door, and I turned around. It was Sarah.

"Hey, I'm sorry for dropping in while you're waiting for you sister, but after everything that happened last night,

I thought you could use the company. Truth be told, I could too."

I walked over to her and threw my arms around her. She buried her head in my chest again and held on to me as tight as she could. We both cried again in the hallway right outside my room, and I put my forehead against the top of her head. Suddenly, someone wrapped their arms around the both of us. I looked up, and Dean was there.

"Hey!" I yelled, wiping the tears off my face.

"I'm really sorry for what happened to her, bro," he said. "I know she meant a lot to you."

I nodded in agreement and thanked him for coming down to check on me.

"I wish things could be different," I told them. "I love you guys. Even though I leave today, I don't want you guys to forget about that."

"We're proud of you," Sarah said. "We are so proud of you."

"Larry," a nurse called. I looked up at her. "Blake and Emily are waiting for you outside the unit in the lobby."

I looked at the two of them. The best friends I could have ever asked for in recovery, the friends I knew would be there for me for the rest of my life when I needed them. I had their phone numbers, so I knew I could stay in touch. Before I left, the three of us had one more group hug. I knew I would have to let go, but all that was in me was telling me to hold on to them and to not let them out of my arms.

"Okay, get outta here," Sarah said as she wiped a few tears from her face with the sleeve of her hoodie. I shook Dean's hand and kissed Sarah on the forehead and picked up my bags and headed for the door.

The second I saw Emily and Blake, I ran up to them and threw my arms around them both.

"It's so good to be bringing you home," Emily said. Dr. Smith had told them everything that happened, so they knew how I felt.

"Let's go home," I said as tears rolled down my face.

Blake patted me on the back. "You look so good," he told me.

I sat in the back seat of Emily's car while Blake sat in the passenger seat. The cold air of Princeton felt a lot colder, yet the sun beaming through the window of the car felt just as warm. As we pulled out of that parking lot, I looked up at the windows of Six North and saw Sarah standing in the window, waving me goodbye. I pulled out my phone and texted her, "We're celebrating when you get discharged." Even though I knew she wouldn't see that until tonight.

As we drove down the same roads Lucy and I walked just a week ago, I couldn't help but feel my heart sink into my chest a second time. The world shone a little less bright now that she was gone.

## CHAPTER 30

I stood at the foot of Lucy's grave shortly after the funeral. I was wearing a suit and tie that I had shortly undone. My hair was gelled and combed down to the side. I had gone to the funeral and sat and talked with Ewan, but for the most part, I stayed quiet during the entire time. It was her family there, so I didn't feel like I should have said much, even though her dad introduced me a lot to different family members.

They didn't lower her casket yet. They normally do that after everyone leaves and while everyone else goes to the reception. I stayed behind to spend time alone with her before I went. I wrote a note I wanted to read at Lucy's funeral but didn't get the chance to. I pulled it out of my suit jacket pocket and opened it up. My hands shook while I faced the reality of how real all this was. I started reading it.

"I met her the day after I started treatment. She was quiet. She didn't say much of anything from how nervous she was, but that night, when she finally opened up, we became so close. By the end of the week, I knew I had to do anything to see her happy. To see her smile and know she was going to be taken care of." Reading this note out loud was making me more emotional than it did when I was writing it. "The night we spent under Princeton's night sky was one of the best nights of my life, and I will hold it close to my heart for the rest of my life. Zach said we are on a road to recovery. Well, if we are on a road to recovery, you were my shotgun rider. Every moment we spent together was completely worth it. Every smile, every kiss, every hard time and pain we spent together in that unit was worth it. Knowing where I stand now and knowing what I know now…I'd do it all over again."

I folded up the note I wrote and tossed it on top of the casket. I put my hand over the top of my eyes to hide the pain I was feeling.

"That was beautiful," I heard a voice say. I got scared and jumped forward a little. When I turned around, I was surprised it was Bill standing there.

"Hey, Pastor," I said. I coughed to clear my scratchy voice. "What are you doing here?"

"Well, since I'm the lead chaplain at the hospital, I make it a priority to be at the funeral of any patient that passes away." I didn't reply. I didn't know what to say. "Even if they're not Catholic, Larry."

That brought an actual smile to my face.

"Larry," he said, "I want to talk to you. Over the time you were at the unit, I've seen you make outstanding progress in recovery. I know that you're not perfect yet, but I'm happy at how far you've made it. I'm worried after what happened with the man you thought was your dad, and now Lucy, that you're going to lose all your progress."

"What would it matter?" I asked.

"Everything!" he replied. He moved in closer to me. "You need to understand that this means everything. God has a plan for your life. We need you here. Your family, your friends. We all do."

"I don't feel like I can stand this," I said. I started to feel down on myself again.

"Then fall on Jesus!" he exclaimed. "The prophet Isaiah said, if you don't stand on faith, you won't stand at all. So if you do need to fall, then fall on the one who will catch you and put you back on your feet."

I nodded in agreement. I knew he was right; I knew I couldn't give up on recovery. I just didn't know how I should be feeling.

Bill put his hands on my shoulders and started praying for me.

"Father, I pray for Larry right now. I know he's in a lot of emotional hurt and this has been an emotional roller coaster for him. But, Father, You can heal every broken heart, and deliverance comes from You and You alone." As he was praying, I started to feel relief. My pain wasn't gone, but I felt comforted while he was praying. I knew I was cared about. "Deliver Larry from what he faces, deliver him from what's tearing him up, and deliver him from his eating disorder. It's in Jesus's name I pray all these things. Amen."

"Thank you," I said.

He pulled out a couple of tissues from his jacket pocket for me to wipe my tears and blow my nose.

"Larry, here's a card with my number and e-mail on it," he said. "I'd love to see you through your discipling process. If you need anything, absolutely anything, you make sure you give me a call."

"I will," I said.

He gave me a hug and patted me on the back a couple of times before he started walking away.

"Hey!" I called out to him. He turned around and looked at me. "How do you keep your faith? With the world we live in and all the betrayal and pain, how can we put our trust in God?"

"Read 2 Corinthians chapter 4, verse 18," he said. "I believe that will answer your question." With that, it was just me alone again. I walked over and kissed my hand and reached out and touched Lucy's casket with it.

"I'll always love you," I said.

After that, I got in my truck and started to drive off.

# CHAPTER 31

I didn't go home after the funeral; I couldn't yet. I went to the beach in Cape May, the same place I promised to take Lucy. It was cold outside, so I took my suit jacket off and put a hoodie on over my dress shirt and tie and replaced my dress shoes with my work boots, which I kept in the back seat of my truck. I began to walk up the cold, quiet beach. The sun was starting to make an appearance, that it was going down soon, but I still had at least two hours left of sunshine. It was quiet, the only sound I could hear the waves crashing against the shore, and all I could see looking out to the ocean were ships in the distance.

This was the same place I walked with Anna months ago, and it was the same place I planned on taking Lucy when she was supposed to get out. I walked down the cold and lonely beach by myself all the way to the jetty that stuck out far into the ocean. When I got to the jetty, I climbed up on top and walked down it about halfway. Now, I was just surrounded by the huge rocks and water. There was a small rock sitting by my feet. Anger started to build up inside me along with the emotion of sadness and loneliness. I picked up that rock and threw it as hard as I could into the ocean and watched it splashed. "Why, God?" I screamed as hard as I could while finding every bit of strength I could to not fall to my knees. "Why? Why did she have to go so soon?" I asked God.

"I thought I'd find you here," I heard someone say. It startled me, and I turned around quickly to put a face to a familiar voice. It was my dad.

"What are you doing here?" I asked. "How did you even find me?" My anger started building up heavier inside. He was the absolute last person I wanted to see.

"I knew you had a funeral for a girl today. Emily told me about it. I went to her house to find you, and she said you weren't home," he said. He walked up and stood next to me and looked out into the ocean with me. "I knew you'd come here. This was always your favorite spot. I remember your mother and me taking you here all the time when you were little."

"Lucy. Her name was Lucy," I said. "Like you care about her, anyway."

"Then her name was Lucy," he said calmly. How calm he was being started to make me calm down a little.

"Okay, but that doesn't answer why you're here," I said. "You're not my dad, so why bother?"

"Because you were right, Larry. I was the closest thing you had to a dad," he said, turning toward me. "I failed you, Larry, and I'm sorry."

I turned from him and started walking back; it was going to take a lot more than a simple apology to make up for everything he'd done to me. It didn't stop him, though. He followed me off the jetty and started keeping up with my pace back up the beach.

"You know what happened after that family therapy session?" he asked.

I stopped walking and turned back to him.

"Yeah, I do know. I emotionally fell apart all over again!" I yelled. "Not like you cared. You didn't even come in and check on me before you left."

"That doctor, your doctor in the unit," he said softly, "he pulled me aside and accused me of being an alcoholic. He said the reason I was angry at you was that I couldn't control my emotions because of it. He said I was drinking my entire life away."

"You were!" I yelled at him. My emotions started to build up again. I could feel anger coming up.

"I didn't believe him, so he told me to go one week without drinking to prove him wrong. But I couldn't," he said. "Larry, I just couldn't. So I called him and asked him for help, and he got me into a two-week rehab for it."

"Did you learn anything?" I asked.

"I learned that I was a horrible person to you. I don't care what happened in the past. It was no excuse for the way I treated you. My therapist helped me to see that too."

"I don't think you realized all the hurt and trauma you caused me," I said.

"I don't," he said. "I don't, but I want to learn. I want to learn more about you. I want to have a father-son bond with you."

"Why?" I asked. "If you're not my dad, then why?"

He didn't speak for a few moments; he turned his head and looked out into the ocean and back to me.

"Because after I realized what I did to you, I felt ashamed. I didn't want to reach out then because I didn't even know where to begin to start asking for your forgiveness. But after your sister told me about your girlfriend that died, I cried. I cried for her, and I cried for you, because I didn't know how badly you were hurting yourself. I knew in my heart that I didn't care how long or how hard I had to push to make things right with you. I needed to make things right with you."

I started crying again, which made him cry.

"It's okay. I'm right here," he said. And he came in and hugged me. I kept my arms to my side, but he hugged me and told me things would be okay. I sucked up my tears, and he let go. I turned aside and looked out into the ocean; he did the same. All I wanted was a relationship with him. Seeing him here right now destroyed me. I didn't know if I should be happy, sad, or angry.

"All this," I said, "this whole thing about healing and working between us, it's going to take time." The old me would have cursed him out and written him off. But Jesus in me was telling me to forgive him. As badly as this was burning me up, I knew I had to.

"And I'm okay with that," he told me. "I know I put you through a lot, son, but I'm looking forward to seeing you grow into a man. A way better man than I ever was or thought I was."

"Where would we even start?" I asked him. "You can't treat me like trash my entire life and expect me to welcome you like nothing happened!" I knew I was supposed to; it was just going to take some work. *I'm not perfect.*

"We could go fishing?" he said and looked at me. I looked at him, and we stared at each other for a moment before we broke out laughing.

"If it makes you feel any better, I wasn't perfect either," I said, chuckling. "I used to steal candy out of your nightstand as a kid."

"That's okay." He chuckled. "I stole some of your Easter candy as a kid a time or two."

"I used to stop the recording of your TV show to watch *SpongeBob*," I said, trying to sound impressive.

"And I threw out your *SpongeBob* DVD when you were little because I was sick of watching it," he said. "Want to continue?" he asked, laughing. I joined his laughter. It was the first time I laughed since Thursday night. It was so hard to believe it was with him.

"I know I failed you growing up," he said, "but if you let me, I want nothing more than to fix everything what I've broken."

"I'd like that," I said. I knew it would take time, but we had to start somewhere.

"I'm so proud of you, son," he told me.

I looked at him and smiled. "That's all I ever wanted to hear from you," I told him, and a tear of happiness ran down my cheek. He walked over and put his arm around my shoulders, and we watched the waters crash on the coast. I'd give anything to have Lucy with us right now, anything.

Zach once said that recovery really starts when we get out of treatment. When there are no nurses watching us use the bathroom, or when there are no staff members watching us eat. He once told us that true recovery starts when we are on our own. He said if we are on the road to recovery, then being in treatment is like sitting at a red light, and when we get out, it's when the light turns green.

I looked at my dad and out into the ocean. I knew there was going to be more mistakes I'd make. I wasn't perfect yet, but I was willing to do whatever I could to get to recovery, and I was ready. For God and for Lucy. *This is for Lucy. The light is green, and I'm going down the road to recovery.*

Ready…and go!

# EPILOGUE

## Winter of 2024

I woke up around six in the morning after arriving. I fell asleep on the couch and from the mixture of the heavy blankets and the fireplace. I bet the temperature outside was freezing. I started brewing a pot of coffee and warmed a piece of pie that was left by the church inside the house, and I went outside to grab the bags I left in my truck.

The cold winter air smacked me in the face the moment I opened the door, and I saw a fresh blanket of snow covering the yard. It filled my footprints from last night. I grabbed my bags and brought them inside as quickly as I could and threw them on the couch and went to check my phone to see a text from both my dad and Sarah wishing me good luck with my new career as a pastor and my fresh start in a different state. I kept the fire going and drank my coffee. It was cold out, so I figured I'd enjoy a fresh cup of coffee and this wonderful pie that was left for me before going out and exploring the new town that I would be pastoring in.

My dad and I had a few bumps, but he became the dad he promised me he'd be, and Sarah, Zach, Dean, and I became extremely close friends over the years. I couldn't have asked for a better group of recovery warriors.

Lucy left me years ago, but the hurt I felt was still there. Every time I close my eyes, I can still see her beautiful eyes and that mesmerizing smile. But I can't stop now. The scripture Bill gave me at her funeral said, "As we look not to the things that are seen but to the things that are unseen. For the things that are seen are transient, but the things that are unseen are eternal" (2 Cor. 4:18 ESV). That's exactly what I need to do. God is watching out for me. God loves me. No matter what road I go down on, I know he's going down it with me. It'll be okay.

I looked outside at the snow, and as beautiful as it was, it was nothing compared to the night we spent together under Princeton's night sky.

I'd love to see it again.

I'd love to see her again.

# AFTERWORD

Since I was a little kid, all the way through high school, I enjoyed reading and writing. After my dad died when I was nine, I started writing to keep my mind off it. I started struggling heavily with bulimia when I was in tenth grade. That was when I first had the idea for this book. Since Larry is loosely based off me, the first time I wrote this book, Larry died before going to treatment, since that was what I thought would happen to me.

After senior year of high school, I tried again and again to write this book, but I couldn't. I don't know why I just couldn't write past the prologue. If I did make it past the prologue, I couldn't make it past the first chapter. I shared this struggle with my friend Mariah, and that year, for Christmas she gave me a journal with a note on it that said, "If you're going to write a book, you'll need something to write in. Merry Christmas." That pushed me to start writing this book again. My friend Kayla and her sister Hannah read my book as I was writing it and gave me constant encouragement and prayer to continue pushing through this. Writing this book brought up a lot of hard memories that I had to pray over as I went through this. I didn't get to mention him in this book, but my brother Wes was one of my best friends during my struggle.

If you are struggling with an eating disorder, I would encourage you and pray that you go to treatment and that you get the help you need. Please do not keep it a secret; do not be afraid to tell on yourself. Keep pushing and fighting for recovery. I pray that you find Jesus, and I pray that He guide and lead you down to recovery.

Most importantly, keep your eyes on eternity.

God bless, my friends.

—Welland Andrus

CPSIA information can be obtained
at www.ICGtesting.com
Printed in the USA
LVHW032038220920
666815LV00003B/214